The $\mathcal{A}$theist Camel
Chronicles

The *A*theist Camel
Chronicles

Debate Themes & Arguments for the Non-Believer
(and those who think they might be)

Dromedary Hump

To Carole-Anne, Josh and Justin,
the people
who give my life meaning.

*"Religion is the most malevolent of all mind viruses.
We should get rid of it as quick as we can."*

—Sir Arthur C. Clarke (1917–2008)

Contents

Introduction

For almost seventeen hundred years, since the Emperor Constantine made Christianity the state religion of Rome, Christianity has grown in power and influence over the Western world. Along with it came abuses of power that were contradictory to the message the figurehead of Christianity was credited with promoting. Wars, persecutions, torture, executions, the breadth and impact of those abuses in God's name are well documented and rival or surpass the genocidal acts of modern day tyrants.

Christianity's hold over European governments steadily declined and was all but a shadow by the end of the 13th century as monarchies shook off the Church's influence. Today, while many European countries claim Christianity as their state religion, it holds no sway over governmental policy. Even the Church's influence on the general population, once absolute, is now viewed largely as quaint suggestions for adherence to outmoded sectarian doctrine, except among the most devout. A poll conducted in 2005 reported that 52% of European Union citizens do not believe in a God, spirit, or life force. Only 20% of Europeans attend church regularly.[1] This downward trend in religiosity represents a remarkable turnabout from what is the seat of Christianity.

In the United States, however, atheists and agnostics represent only 8% to 16% of the populace. Yet, while the upper end of those estimates exceeds the percentage of Jews, African-Americans, and Latinos in the United States, atheists wield little power or influence. The dominance of the Christian faith remains strong not only among the general population, but on the political front. Its adherents exert significant influence over local, state, and federal governmental policy. Its tenets, its dogma, are deep seated among legislators, some Supreme Court justices, within the military, and for eight years under George W. Bush, in the Executive branch. The result has been an attempt to dismember the "Wall of Separation" between religion and government as guaranteed by the First Amendment's establishment clause.

This religious taint has given rise to governmental funding of faith-based charitable initiatives with no oversight as to how the funds are spent, opening the door for taxpayer/ government funded proselytizing. It has influenced the decision making of the FDA, impeding the approval of new birth control drugs. It has attempted to reinstate school prayer and impeded genuine scientific learning with creationist aka Intelligent Design pseudo-science in public schools. It is dedicated to dictating acceptable sexual practices; exerting

---

[1] http://en.wikipedia.org/wiki/Religion_in_the_European_Union

control of familial life and death decisions of pregnant women and the terminally ill; and seeks to subjugate the rights of people whose life style preferences are considered an abomination to their God. Most frightening, the name of their God has been invoked as justification for foreign policy decisions, including those that led us into war in Iraq—shades of the Old Testament's God of the Israelites who led them into battle against pagan neighbors with genocidal results.

Christianity is not alone in the power it holds over the mind of man, and the injustices it provokes. For the past forty years radical Muslim faithful have been waging a war against its fellow Abrahamic religions (Christianity and Judaism) guided by their scripture, in the name of their prophet, and with the blessings of Allah. Some theocratic Islamic nations have purged Hindus from their lands, destroying their ancient temples, declaring them an affront to Islam. Hindu extremists in India threaten the murder of secular Indians who dare to observe the innocuous secular Western tradition of Valentines Day.

In short, religion, specifically fundamentalist religious belief, has transcended its original ancient purpose of establishing and promoting societal mores, solidifying cultures, and proffering supernaturally based answers for the unknown in a pre-scientific age. It has become a source of intolerance, an obstacle to scientific advancement for the betterment of mankind, a tool for intrusion into personal freedoms, and a justification for waging death and destruction all under the banner of a divine dictate. The intolerant and provocative texts and doctrine of the three major monotheistic religions have caused misery for thousands of years. But with the advent of the nuclear age their dogma, their scripture, specifically Christianity's and Islam's with their promise of a better world with the destruction of this one, represents a real and present threat.

This is not to say that all theists are evil. It's my experience that the majority of believers are good, fair, and reasonable folks whose beliefs give them personal comfort. Most that I know, and all those that I love, abhor the excesses and rigidity of their fundamentalist brethren, and understand the necessity of the separation of church and state. I bear no ill will toward those people regardless of their preferred belief system, even while I find their clinging to superstition archaic and irrational. However, if they fail to speak up and against their fundamentalist fanatical counterparts and the threat they represent to all of us, then they are a part of the problem not part of the solution.

Thanks to atheist activists like Richard Dawkins, Christopher Hitchens, Sam Harris and others, where atheistic thought was once kept hidden usually by necessity, it has now come out into the open although still far from being perceived as a positive attribute by the believer majority. While the voices of the Free Thinkers grow there is as of this writing still only one avowed atheist in the US Congress. A recent poll reported that most US citizens said they'd vote for an openly homosexual Muslim before they'd cast their vote for a Godless atheist. There are still state laws held over from the 18th & 19th centuries that deny atheists the right to hold public office, albeit they have been declared unconstitutional by the Supreme Court and thus not enforced.

These essays are a collection of my perspectives of the human condition as impacted by religion. They were prompted by debates and discussions with theists online and in person; news articles/current events; religious blog postings; and my observations of society at large. Many of the arguments I proffer are in response to timeless theistic fallacies. Others are a product of, response to, modern turns in religious thinking or theist activism.

I am not a scientist; I only play one in chat rooms and message boards. But I admire the contributions that science has made to civilization. I respect the scientific method. I have no "faith" in anything in the religious sense of the word. Indeed, I reject the concept of faith as a theological construct. That I fully expect the sun will rise in the east tomorrow isn't a matter of my having faith, it's a matter of possessing a basic understanding of cosmology, general observation, and statistical probability. Thus, in lieu of mindless faith I possess a high level of *confidence* that the sun will rise in the east—yet again—tomorrow.

I do not claim to speak for all non-believers. Atheists are a varied lot. We share no common dogma or doctrine. We share only the lack of belief in God or gods. My opinions are offered as food for thought to the atheist, agnostic, skeptic, and to those theists whose tie to the ancient superstitions is in conflict with their refusal to simply ignore 21st century rationality. If this book prompts discourse, encourages activism, promotes debate, or simply stimulates questioning of previously held perspectives, then my best hopes for it will have been realized.

1

I Am Not a Skeptic

01 Jan 2008

Skep·tic

– noun 1. a person who questions the validity or authenticity of something purporting to be factual.

2. a person who maintains a doubting attitude, as toward values, plans, statements, or the character of others.

3. a person who doubts the truth of a religion, esp. Christianity, or of important elements of it.[1]

Best we get this cleared up from the start: I am not a skeptic on matters pertaining to the supernatural, God, gods, Satan, angels, et al.

I don't *question* the validity of the supernatural; I reject it entirely at face. I don't *doubt* the truth of any religion; I utterly dismiss it as mindlessness, antiquated thought process and a means of mind enslavement.

---

[1] http://dictionary.reference.com/browse/skeptic

I am no more a skeptic on these topics than I am skeptical about alien autopsies or abductions, the living dead, mind readers, fortune tellers, or ghosts. I utterly reject and dismiss them as fantasies borne either from the imaginations, or mental infirmities of people.

My skepticism is reserved for things that could be real but are dubious, such as a stranger who claims to have multiple sets of genitalia. Could it be so? Absolutely. Genetic mutations, genetic damage, can produce multiple sexual organs, mixed sex organs, or the lack of genitalia entirely. But, I'd be skeptical of his claim as the frequency of such occurrences is miniscule, and because it's unlikely that a stranger would want to divulge such information voluntarily and unprompted.

I'll also save my skepticism for scientific theory for which there has been insufficient evidence testing or study, no corroboration, or failure to repeat said findings in controlled conditions. It's possible that the theory could be true if it has some basis in natural law, or promotes a new "natural" event or condition not yet known. String Theory is such an example. I'll reserve buy in, I'll be skeptical, until more evidence, and scientifically accepted conditions are satisfied.

But God, gods, angels, demons, devil, heaven, hell, people formed from dust or ribs, the dead rising, water walking, transformation of water into an alcohol, millions of animal species on a boat, etc., etc., defies Man's experience, observations and understanding of natural law. It has no visible means of scientific support. I am not skeptical about it having occurred; *I reject it entirely.* I am a person who respects the laws of the natural universe and whose thinking is grounded in reality.

Please, don't call me a religious skeptic. To quote Katherine Hepburn: *"I'm an atheist and that's it."*

2

Why Christians Aren't "CHRISTians" At All

03 Jan 2008

The Christian Bible includes the Hebrew Bible, the Tanakh. Christians refer to it as the Old Testament. Most scholars agree that the Hebrew Bible was composed and compiled between the 12th and the 2nd century BCE. Jesus and his disciples based their teachings on the Tanakh, referring to its tenets as *"… the law of Moses, the prophets, and the psalms … the scriptures"*. (Luke 24:44–45).

In it are contained more than six hundred laws that establish how to conduct ones secular and religious life, which in ancient times were undistinguishable from each other. These laws are very strict, requiring stoning of unruly children, stoning of homosexuals, killing of adulteresses, eating kosher foods, circumcision of male children, etc. The list is long and detailed.

As a devout Jew, and rabbi, Jesus himself would have followed these laws. He may have been at odds with the Jewish priestly class who didn't hold themselves accountable to the law, or who enforced laws that Jesus felt were being misinterpreted/misapplied, such as the admonishment against the poor gleaning fields on the Sabbath. But Judaism, by definition, requires reverence for and obedience to *"the law of Moses, and the prophets."* To abandon those laws would be to abandon the very foundation of the Jewish religion. Jesus never did that.

How do I know? Jesus is alleged to have said so himself:

"For truly, I say to you, till heaven and earth pass away, not an iota, not a dot, will pass the law until all is accomplished. Whoever then relaxes one of the least of these commandments and teaches men so shall be called least in the kingdom of heaven; but he who does them and teaches them shall be called great in the kingdom of heaven." (Matthew 5:18-19 RSV)

He makes similar declarations at least two more times in Luke 16:17 and Matthew 5:17.

The earliest Christians were Jews. They followed the laws of Moses and the Prophets, as did Jesus himself along with revering Jesus' teachings – a reformed Judaism.

Yet, when you ask a Christian why they ignore and disobey the Old Testament laws, they give you this song and dance: *"Oh… that's the OLD Testament. There's a new covenant with God; Jesus did away with the old laws."* Nope, not true as shown above in Jesus' own words. But their justification for this abandonment of God's laws is this: *"For Christ is the end of the law, that every one who has faith may be justified."* (Romans 10:4)

But Romans was written by Paul. It was not dictated by Jesus, not hinted at by Jesus, not referenced in any pre-Paulian scripture. It's Paul's abandonment of Jewish law to make the Christian cult more palatable to the gentile (pagan Roman) recruits. It's in direct contradiction to Jesus' multiple admonishments. It's not by coincidence Paul included it in his letter to the Romans. Let's face it; requiring circumcision to join the cult would have certainly put a crimp in the recruitment plan.

So why don't Christians follow Jesus' words, keep kosher, kill witches on sight, and get circumcised, etc., etc.? Because they find it easier, more convenient, to follow Paul than they do their professed Lord and Savior. They aren't Christians at all; they are Paulists. They follow a false prophet, and they, along with Paul, "… *shall be called the least in the kingdom of heaven.*"

One can imagine that when they croak, and Jesus smells that bacon on their breath, and gets a glimpse of their foreskins, they are truly screwed.

3

Give Us Just One Certifiable Miracle!

06 Jan 2008

Five million sick, crippled and desperate pilgrims visit Lourdes France each year seeking miraculous healing relief. But, in the past one hundred-fifty years the Catholic Church has recognized only sixty-seven "miracle" healings. Sixty-seven out of millions upon millions of sick prayerful faithful! Interestingly, not one of those sixty-seven was an amputee. Why?

There are roughly 360 million amputees on Earth. Thirty-three percent of the Earth's population is Christian. Let's broadly assume that approximately one-third of those 360 million amputees are Christians. That's roughly 120 million Christian amputees.

Out of those 120 million Christians alive today, forgetting the millions of Christian amputees who preceded them, how many of them at anytime in their lives prayed over and over to Jesus to have their amputated limbs miraculously restored? My guess is a lot. But, let's be conservative in our estimate and say one third of them, 40 million, prayed for full restoration of their missing limb(s).

Yet, of those 40 million living Christian amputees who prayed for God to restore their missing appendages not one—NOT ONE—has ever had that prayer answered in the affirmative.

How do I know this? Because spontaneous regeneration of a human limb, akin to a starfish sprouting a new arm, would be published in every reputable medical journal, headlined in every print media, be all over the internet, broadcast over every radio, TV, and shortwave frequency on the planet. Every doctor and scientist on the planet would be examining this special event with every known piece of technology at their disposal. The churches would be playing it up, praising the Lord till their crucifixes and prayer beads were rubbed to nubs. But no, not a single occurrence, ever.

So, once again the obvious questions remain:

> ➤ Why not a single limb regeneration in spite of Jesus' promises that all prayers of the faithful will be answered?

> ➤ Were the prayers answered, but in the negative … EVERY TIME? If so, is it because God hates amputees?

> ➤ Or didn't a single one of these 40 million prayerful Christians, and their predecessors, have enough faith to gain God's favor and elicit Jesus' merciful healing power?

Christians are quick to point to anecdotal instances of miraculous prayer healing of so-and-so's hemorrhoids, or so-and-so's back pain, or some relative's cancer going into remission (as so many cancer patients undergoing treatment do). But this amputee thing is problematic for them. They actually get angry when it is posed to them.

The usual dodge is: *"God doesn't just dispense healing like a drink dispenser;"* or *"God is testing their faith";* or *"It's God's will; who are we to question?";* or *"God looks at things in ways we can't comprehend.";* or *"Being an amputee builds character."* (Evidently a raging case of hemorrhoids isn't a character-building infirmity.) Tired old platitudinous denials invoked to avoid confronting that fearful, faith-shattering reality they dare not confront.

Thus, they will go on making up excuses, referring to their apologetics sites, baaing their devotion, defending the indefensible, blaming atheists for this *"ridiculous argument,"* and refusing to deal with the problem head on when all along the ugly truth is staring them in the face.

4

US Theocracy: Threat or Paranoia?

10 Jan 2008

In the 1930's the Jews in Germany refused to believe that their German heritage and patriotism wouldn't be as respected as that of the gentile majority, their neighbors. They were blind to the coming storm that would result in the dissolution of their rights, subjugation, enslavement and eventual extermination.

Likely few moderate Muslims in Iran under the Shah ever expected the day would come when a secular government would be dissolved; or in Afghanistan under the Taliban that women would be whipped in the streets for not covering their heads and faces; that freedoms they took for granted would be banned, that the religious extremists would dictate the law and culture they would follow.

When the Puritans left England because they objected to the Anglican Church's suppression of their particular minority religious beliefs, did they ever foresee themselves eventually emulating the same intolerance, hanging Quakers, persecuting Baptists and shunning those who dared to question their Puritan supremacy?

Examples of the injustice and intolerance caused by theocracies, or by governments that endorsed the prevailing religious majority's demonizing of "the other" is well documented by many more examples through history. The Founding Fathers saw the evils of a theocracy—the Church's entanglement in the monarchies of Europe—and remembered well the excesses that religious exclusionism of the ruling majority wreaked on the minority.

While many of the Founding Fathers were Deists, the majority of them were Christians. Nevertheless, they had the foresight and impartiality to put their individual beliefs aside long enough to forge a guideline that would ensure that no one's particular thoughts on religion would be forced upon, nor preferred over, anyone else's beliefs; that the impartiality of government in religious matters would always protect the minority, "the other". This was such an important issue that it was codified in the First Amendment to the Constitution and reconfirmed by the Supreme Court time and again since the first challenge to it in 1947.

There are people today who want to distort, pervert, and even change the meaning of that law. They want to declare majority rule of their religious belief. They want to establish a country where if you're not part of their belief system you ARE the "other," and you can either "love it or leave it." A nation where you either embrace Jesus as your savior and march to their concept of their supreme deity's "true and righteous" code of laws and culture, or you become an outcast. Some want a constitutional amendment to declare this a "Christian Nation" in direct opposition to the Founding

Fathers' vision. [*Google* "Christian Nation Amendment" for more information on this movement.]

Some of these people are already serving in government in high positions, thanks to appointments by the two Bush administrations; Supreme Court Justices Scalia, Alito, Thomas and Roberts being among the most obvious, onerous and odious.

Most Americans will say, *"Nonsense, that's paranoia."* or *"That isn't going to happen here... this is America!"* or worst and most frightening of all, *"So what's so bad if we put Jesus back in the schools?"*

It won't happen suddenly where you wake up and there's a cross on our flag, and a crucifix above the county court house; or you find a tax notice in your mailbox for espousing an opposing belief or no belief at all, ala Muslim countries; or you find Evolution is banned from public school curricula. No, it will be slower and much more insidious. It's happening already. *God on Trial* by Peter Irons exposes the thinking of these fanatics as they wage war in our courts against secular government. Your blood will run cold when you read the mentality and and objectives of the Religious Right in their own words; the challenges to the Establishment Clause to promote religiosity on public lands, in schools and government buildings; and their commitment to extinguish our 225 year secular history. Make yourself aware. Know who you're voting for. If it's someone who says they are a "Christian Leader," be afraid. If he says he will follow the word of God, before the rule of law, be VERY afraid.

I wonder if things in Europe would have been different for the Jews of the 30's and 40's if they had been just a bit more paranoid, and remembered the past. As Santayana said, *"Those who cannot remember the past are condemned to repeat it."*

Invariably a Christian will ask: *"What percentage of the Christians who believe this should be a Christian nation would be in favor of religious freedom? What percentage do you think would be in favor of restricting religious freedom?"*

Is it Christians' outright denial or their ignorance of history that prompts such questions? There are no statistics that will answer their questions. But, what we do have is a thousand years of history. What that history shows us is this:

➢ Where a government endorsed a single religion those of dissenting belief are/were treated differently, and badly. Church of England, any of the Catholic European monarchies, czarist Russia, Iran, Saudi Arabia, the Taliban; even Israel elevates their Jewish citizens above Muslim Israelis.

➢ Christianity has shown remarkable intolerance toward other beliefs, or people who lack belief. Huguenots, Calvinists, Martin Luther, The Catholic Church were prime instigators of terror and persecution of citizens not of their religious flavor. Cathars, Coptic Christians, Jews, Muslims and atheists, were among their targets. More recently, Brigham Young, Fred Phelps, Billy Graham, Pat Robertson, Jerry Falwell, Ted Haggard and President George H.W. *("I don't think atheists are patriots or even Americans")* Bush, have demonstrated how they feel about those who don't hold their preferred beliefs.

➢ Minority Christian sects who have felt the oppression of the majority Christian sect and left to escape their persecutors (i.e. the Puritans, Dutch Catholics) invariably established their own intolerance toward and persecution of those outside their sect.

But the ultimate question to those who profess Americans' freedoms would be untouched by a Christian theocracy is this: *If in declaring the US a "Christian Nation" there is no disadvantage to the minority (atheists, Jews, Hindus, Wiccans, Moslems, et al) and no advantage for the majority (Christians), <u>then what possible purpose does declaring the US a Christian nation serve?</u>*

I, for one, don't wish to see the US as a testing ground for the hypothesis that Christians are now a kinder gentler people and theocracy a benign and un-prejudiced system of government. There is no evidence for it. The motto *"In God We Trust"* is bad enough; we can do without *"In Our God You Trust ...Or Else!"*

5

"Truth" and truth

12 Jan 2008

The word truth is rather unambiguous, and never capitalized unless it is the first word of a sentence. Yet, theists and spiritualists seem to insist on capitalizing the word, and imbuing it with some mystical sense.

Verifiable fact is truth. Reality is truth. Honesty is truth. The truth of a matter can be discovered with knowledge that stems from the scientific method, observation, repeatability in controlled conditions, corroborating cumulative evidence, and/or by a preponderance of objective evidence.

This "Truth" theists refer to (with a capital "T") is a spiritualist invention, just like "sin," just like "resurrection," just like "the Rapture." It has no valid meaning outside the world of spiritualism and religious think. There can be no "truth" in "faith" since faith is by definition not rooted in evidence, proofs or verifiability. That's why it's called "faith".

Their "Truth," much like their "God," is useless outside of their own sphere of mindset. Much like a "Tribble" (a mythical fur-bearing critter from the early *Star Trek* TV show) would have no significance to an astronaut or astrophysicist.

Defining "God" is much easier. It's the fictional thing that people, whose minds are infected by ancient pre-scientific belief systems, believe controls their lives, created the universe, endows them with an after-life as a reward for their belief, and/or controls volcanic eruptions, rain fall, solar and lunar eclipses, success at hunting, crop yield, births, disease outbreaks, victory in war, Aunt Sadie's cancer, lotto results, and the outcome of sporting competitions, etc., ad nauseam.

These unfortunate and religiously impaired people are typically indoctrinated to their belief in their god by their parents and assume the prevailing god definition of their culture. Although many are capable of intelligence and reason in many other areas of human endeavor, the "religious meme" prevents most of them from breaking free of this indoctrination. It's a powerful meme. And *that's* the truth.

6

Jesus and the Pigs

15 Jan 2008

Mathew 8:28-34 gives an account of Jesus purging demons from two men who were possessed. In it the demons beg Jesus not to send them into the abyss, but instead to allow them to infest a herd of pigs. Jesus agrees. The demons promptly leave the men to enter the pigs, which promptly run amok, throw themselves over a cliff into a lake and die.

In discussing this weird tale with a fundie, he said it wasn't Jesus who was at fault for the loss of the pigs, *"technically it was the demons fault for asking."* Now there's an example of twisted apologetics. It certainly isn't supported by logic. Let's analyze the alleged event.

What are we to believe? That Jesus wasn't powerful enough to do the exorcism without providing a suitable alternate host for the evil spirits? That we have a man-god who takes requests from demons as to how they should be dealt with? Evidently Jesus values the requests of demons over the lives of innocent pigs, not to mention demonstrating a complete disregard for the financial loss to the pig's uninvolved owners.

Putting the fundie's flawed logic in contemporary terms: It would be tantamount to a policeman getting the drop on two known murderers, whom he caught in the act of committing a new murder. The murderers ask the cop not to shoot or arrest and imprison them, but rather to provide them with a lower life form to slaughter in place of their human victim. In response, the cop offers them the two Irish Setters strolling down the sidewalk.

Even if in the course of dispatching the two dogs, the killers managed to kill themselves, my guess is the owner of those dogs, and the judge hearing the suit, would have a lot of questions, not the least of which would be why an authority, empowered and equipped to dispose of the criminals in a sanctioned manner, saw fit to acquiesce to the criminals' request and provide them with substitute victims that belonged to an uninvolved third party.

It takes a pretty good imagination, a fanciful embellishment of the scenario, or serious psychological infirmity to come up with a justification, "technically" or otherwise, that would exonerate the cop and not find him derelict of duty, complicit in the act and fully liable.

Evidently, along with his disdain for "fags" (per Fred Phelps) and figs [Mark 11:12-14], Jesus also hates pigs. And much like the donkey he had his henchmen "borrow" for him [Mathew 21:2], he's not at all concerned about taking or destroying other people's property.

Destroying fig trees, stealing donkeys, killing pigs and setting family members against each other, all clearly indicate a history of sociopathic behavior. Maybe that's why he was ultimately crucified. Sounds like he had it coming.

7

Religion's War on Science Marches On

18 Jan 2008

*"Catholicism and Catholic Universities have always been
the center of scientific advancement."*

This perversion of history almost sent me into spasms. Needless to say, it was uttered by a Catholic whose brain had been steam cleaned by too many Catholic apologetics web pages.

One need only think of Galileo's trial and the threat of imprisonment for heresy; the suppression of Copernicus' writings; and the live incinerations of Michael Servetus, and Giordano Bruno – all at the hands of, or agreement by, the learned Catholic church – to put that nonsense to rest. Even Gregor Mendel's papers, which were left in the monastery after his death, were burned by the succeeding abbot (Personal stupidity or Church directive? One can only speculate). While Catholic apologists (read: revisionists) insist it's all blown out of proportion, the written records of the Church say otherwise.

If Catholic/Christian opposition to scientific discovery had ceased in the 17th century I'd be finished here. But it hasn't. It continues to this day.

Of late, the war against science by the spiritually impaired is over animal cloning. If and when cloning can be reliably and economically implemented, this technology could dramatically increase animal product productivity, ease world hunger, and improve the lot of millions. Unfortunately the cloning of specific animals that are high yield egg, wool, meat, or milk producers, somehow displeases God and/or Its disciples.

Statistics indicate that 79% of Protestants, and 61% of Catholics oppose animal cloning. Of non-believers only 40% oppose it.[1] It's no coincidence, and no surprise either, that the higher the education, and the higher the income level of the poll respondents, the more likely they are to approve of animal cloning.

Some theists like to credit God, and not scientists or doctors, for discoveries that have enhanced or extended our lives. Interestingly, more often than not God gets credit for those things many years after the fact, after theists had opposed the innovation to begin with.(i.e. "If man had been intended to fly, God would have given him wings!"). But, if God is the inspiration for those things theists ultimately come to accept as good, why does God not get blamed for discoveries and technological developments theists deem as bad? If all creative innovation is God's will, why oppose it? Who is to say what "God Hath Wrought" is bad? Or perhaps scientists developing cloning are being given the formula by "Satan!?!?" The brains of believers work in strange and mysterious ways.

---

[1] http://abcnews.go.com/sections/scitech/DailyNews/poll010816_cloning.html

So, religiosity continues its opposition to Man's advancement, and once again stands in the way of the improvement of the human condition. One can only imagine what scriptural chapter and verse Christians will pervert to justify their objections to cloning on religious grounds. As far as I know one has yet to be offered. How about:

"Let no one be found among you...who practices divination or sorcery, interprets omens, engages in witchcraft, or casts spells, or who is a medium or spiritist or who consults the dead. Anyone who does these things is detestable to the LORD..." (Deuteronomy 18: 10-12).

Or better yet: *"The poor you will always have with you."* (Matthew 26:11)

8

MLK, Jr. and an Opportunity Lost

20 Jan 2008

Martin Luther King Jr. Day was established to commemorate the preeminent leader of the Civil Rights movement. His name has become synonymous with the principle of non-violent protest and the struggle for equal rights for all. He will for all time be honored as a martyr for that great cause, and fittingly so.

King's efforts were at the forefront of a freedom movement, committed to free people from the oppression of discrimination. Free them from the injustice of segregation. Free them to exercise the same rights that the Founding Fathers reserved only for the white majority. It represented the final transformation from slavery to first class citizenship.

But, what he failed to do, which he was positioned to do, was to spearhead the final step of freedom for his people: Emancipation from the slavery of the White Man's religious myth.

Ninety-one percent of African Americans compared to 88% of White Americans describe themselves as religious.[1] While not a dramatic discrepancy, one can't ignore the well-established fact that there is a high correlation between religiosity and lower income. Twenty-five percent of Blacks in the US live below the poverty level, twice the rate of Whites.[2]

Victims of their slave ancestors acceptance of the White culture's prevailing Christianity, African Americans have for 200 years been a favored target of televangelist fakes, tent preacher charlatans, faith healers and even cult leaders (Jim Jones' suicide denomination was predominantly Black).

If, as James Madison said, *"Religious bondage shackles and debilitates the mind and unfits it for every noble enterprise, every expanded prospect"* then the very last thing an undereducated, poverty-ridden, newly freed people need are the shackles of religious mind slavery, much less the drain on their finances or distraction from secular self interest that invariably comes along with it. Prayers to Jesus to win the lottery, or to deliver a financial windfall; or to rely on the promise of "pie in the sky by and by when you die" as a reward for their poverty in this life, is at best repressive and at worst mind bondage. It works in direct opposition to self reliance, ambition and personal responsibility, all qualities necessary to maximize potential, rise above and be freed from poverty.

Unfortunately, Dr. King himself was religiously enslaved, and could never have seen or accepted the

---

[1] http://www.ksg.harvard.edu/saguaro/communitysurvey/results2.html

[2] http://www.census.gov/hhes/www/poverty/poverty05/pov05hi.html

fact that it represented one of the last great barriers to Black progress. So much the loss.

Butterfly McQueen, the famed African-American actress understood this when she said: *"As my ancestors are free from slavery, I am free from the slavery of religion."*

9

Why Words are the Enemy of Christians

26 Jan 2008

Have you ever noticed that whenever a word in the Bible causes a problem for theists they will write a full page or more to try and explain away, reinvent new meaning or otherwise distort its usage in order to suit their needs? There must be literally millions of pages of apologetics written by Christians trying to squirm their way out of the embarrassing and contradictory statements that the Bible saddles them with. In this case, a problem related to the human form and all of its ugly functions.

I recently asked a Christian: *"Since Man was made in God's 'image", does this mean God has a penis? And if so, what does he use it for, and on whom?"* Not very original, I know, but the replies are always fun to watch.

He comes back with this: *"Image doesn't mean physical attributes; it means the 'character' of god."* He attaches a link to a few thousand word apologetics article that disassociates the word image from appearance. It's clear this problem has been plaguing believers for some time, as they've devoted an awful lot of inventive thought to it.

This creative redefinition of common words as a way to escape a problem has its own pitfalls. When God said *"thou shalt not make unto thee any graven IMAGES"* it was clear he meant nothing other than what "images" means: physical likenesses, statues, idols, engravings, etchings, paintings, etc. God could not have meant the "character" of graven images ... image meant image.

But you can find apologetics pages that will twist and turn and try escape clauses for that as well. It seems that god of theirs just can't quite get his message across clearly enough for people to understand without a lot of redefinition, helpful assumptions, obfuscation, denial and just plain invention.

Is this because their God is an inarticulate oaf, or because those ancients who invented God didn't expect people would actually question and analyze their inventive stories?

And yet, even if the intent of "image" in the Genesis story was "character," while "image" in the Exodus story was "physical attribute," then the problem becomes even more twisted: If Adam and Eve were created in God's *character,* and since their character shows them to be disobedient miscreants who sinned, it thus stands to reason that their creator is also a miscreant sinner or has the capacity to sin.

If Adam and Eve had the character to do both good and evil, then by definition their creator must have the character to also be good and evil (sinful) since they share common characteristics. So much for the "perfect" god concept; unless by perfect they mean God is both perfectly evil *and* perfectly good. He certainly can't be perfectly good alone, for how does a perfectly good "character" create beings in his image/character that sin?

Oh what a tangled web they weave when first they practice the apologetics of myth.

10

Marketing Jesus: The Selling of a Deity

30 Jan 2008

I've never understood this strange need Evangelical and hardcore Christians have to advertise and promote Christianity; T-shirts, "Chick tracts," bumper stickers, roadside signs, catchy phrases, Church advertisements, etc. But for sheer annoyance, nothing beats the one-on-one *"Have you heard the Good news?"* idiocy of the door-to-door recruiter. (*"Yeah, the good news is my pitbull hates your polyester suit, skinny tie and white socks."*)

They are selling a product. They may as well be promoting a soft drink, or cake frosting, or a candidate running for office. Difference is, the cake frosting label doesn't threaten you with eternal punishment by the great Betty Crocker in The Sky for buying Pillsbury's, or for preferring your cake unfrosted

Sure, fundies interpret the charge of Jesus to go forth and preach the good news as their duty. They want do his PR work, but they don't want to do it on their client Jesus' terms. If they *really* want to play apostle/recruiter and ensure a heavenly reward for their efforts, they should sell all their belongings, give the money to the poor, leave their family, then follow Jesus and shoot their mouths off to anyone who wishes to tolerate it. After all, isn't that what the Bible said Jesus endorsed (Math. 19:21, Mark 10:21, Luke 18:22)?

But, oh no ... that'll never do. Poverty may have been okay for Jesus and his crew, but the guy at the gate of the NASCAR track isn't going let ole Evangelical Jethro in for free.

So, here's my advice to fundies: If you're not willing to go all in, walk the walk, and do it like Jesus told you, then practice your faith without shoving it at people; pray in private and not in public like a hypocrite (Jesus said that too); and leave everyone else the hell alone.

11

On Belief and Respect

02 Feb 2008

I recently heard an atheist say he had more respect for Theist A's religious belief, than he did for Theist B's belief. While they were both forms of Christianity, one of them evidently was worthy of higher respect than the other.

What exactly entitles theistic beliefs to any degree of respect?

> ➢ Is it based on which flavor of unsupportable, culturally-induced sky daddy they worship; what supernatural or inventive illogic they use to support that belief; what dogma they pick and choose from the menu of belief; how deeply they believe it; how effectively they induct their young?

> ➢ Is it whether or not they are a threat to Free Thinkers, or our freedoms, or the education of the young, or the advancement of science, or civilization as a whole?

> ➢ Should we respect a belief just because it is benign, less confrontational, doesn't require witch

burning (any more), doesn't promote hatred of Jews (as much), or the killing of apostates?

➢ Is their belief due the same, less, or more respect as people who believe in unicorns and faeries; the "miracle" of images of holy figures on their sandwiches; that aliens built the pyramids; or who believe the world is 6,000 years old and that men rode dinosaurs?

I once had some New Ager tell me he respected all beliefs. When backed against a wall, he agreed he'd even respect a resurgence of Aztec belief including human sacrifice. Why? Because *"Belief is due respect, because it's a belief."* Ridiculous.

Frankly, I have zero respect for any blind belief, whether it's the hybrid kinder gentler version, or the basic model. Belief in anything with no evidence is self delusion and unworthy of my respect. I'd have the same lack of respect for an atheist's belief if that belief was that he was abducted by aliens.

Now, don't confuse my lack of respect for belief as a justification for being disrespectful to the believer. There are a lot of believers for whom I have respect in spite of their unfortunate enslavement to fable. They have other redeeming qualities. And, I would stand up for their right to believe whatever absurdity they so desire, just so long as it is legal, doesn't impinge on my rights, or threaten society.

It's the 21st century, the scientific age, an age that should be devoted to reason and logic. So, what logic should I be using to have "respect" for belief that is steeped in superstition, ignorance, medieval thinking and the rejection of reality? Sorry, can't think of any.

12

Denying Atheists Exist & Other Proofs of Theist Self Delusion

04 Feb 2008

"ATHEISTS HATE THE TRUE GOD"
"ATHEISTS DELIBERATELY REJECT GOD"
"ATHEISTS PROVE THE EXISTENCE OF GOD BY THEIR OWN LABEL"
"ATHEISTS CREATE CRIMINAL SOCIETIES"
"ATHEISTS ARE THE COMPUTER HACKERS"

These laughable subject headers are what pass for intelligent reasoning among the religiously fanatical. They can be viewed online in all their muddled glory and detailed prose, a testament to theist illogic and self-delusion: http://www.tencommandments.org/heathens2.shtml

A cursory review of these wild ranting essays displays tragically flawed logic, fraught with logical fallacies; circular thinking; self-serving hypotheticals; straw man arguments; statements offered as fact without evidence; and bizarre tangents into pseudo-science.

All lack even the most basic understanding of how to frame, express and prove a hypothesis.

Transparently sophomoric and humorous to thinking people, it underscores the remarkable ability for fanatical theist self delusion, to the point where arguments of the absurd take the place of reason. We the thinking readily dismiss it as representative of the imbalanced theistic mind, and their rejection of reason and reality. But, among the most credulous, unsophisticated, least educated of theist sheep, this stuff is eaten up like silage in a trough. Likely, after reading each paragraph (out loud, with lips moving) they bleat *"Praise Jeeesus!!"* or *"Hallelujah!"* as is their wont.

I won't bother to refute point-by-point all the absurdities of these inane statements. It's unworthy of the exercise. But, if we examine the first two or three premises taken on the whole the point is proven. They infer atheists can't possibly *not* believe in a God. That atheists believe God exists, we just hate him/it. And what's more, the very existence of atheists proves God exists.

To refute and dispel these statements one need only to substitute the phrase *"Werewolf Non-Believer"* for atheist, and *"Werewolf"* for God. Thus, all people really believe in Werewolves, Werewolf Non-Believers just hate them. And they hate them deliberately. Further, the very existence of people who say they are Werewolf Non-Believers proves Werewolves exist. Therefore, there can be no true Werewolf Non-Believers. Q.E.D. Werewolves ARE!

It all makes perfect sense, or at least it does to deluded rubes who genuinely believe in Werewolves or God/gods and devote their lives to them, trying to convince others of them, while trying to win God's or

Werewolf's favor. To those of us who reject werewolves, gnomes, Santa, the Tooth Fairy, God, gods, and all such supernaturalism as the invention of man's fertile imagination, it just sounds absurd.

Unfortunately, to the profoundly religious, sounding absurd is part of the dogma.

13

Modern Day Inquisition: Hump Roast
Rests in Jury's Hands

06 Feb 2008

Ah, the bad old days, when religion was THE guid-
ing force of Men's lives, their governance, their
sole understanding of the World, the only true
source of information.

We call that period The Dark Ages. Fear not, The
Dark Ages isn't over yet!!! Here's Proof.

Sounding very much like the lead prosecutor for
The Inquisition the following comment was left by an
irate Christian on a popular religious blog.

*"Hump, as we have seen, is always about human reason-
ing and getting a response. He has a need to analyze and box
things up tight and neat so the world makes sense to him ...
that is why he does not need a relationship with Jesus, because
he already has everything figured out". ..."* [secular] *books
are not needed for me because I understand the things of the
Kingdom which have nothing to do with human understanding – Prov. 3:5-6."*

So, with that indictment of me let The Inquisition begin!

Inquisitor: "As to Charge Number One: *'always being about Human Reasoning'*, how does the defendant camel plead?"

Hump: "<u>Guilty</u>, Your Grand Inquisitorship."

I confess that I have employed reasoning my entire life. I have called upon my reasoning ability to assess the things I am told and discern the difference between logic and illogic; fact from fiction; evidence from unsupported myth; reality from imagination.

Inquisitor: "As to Charge Number Two: *'using analysis to understand the world'*, how does the defendant camel plead?"

Hump: "<u>Guilty</u>, Your Holi-mess."

I confess that when presented with a statement, an opinion, a "belief," or a hypothesis proffered as fact, I use my analytical ability to weight that input to assess its validity or degree of likelihood. I do so based on my prior experiences, corroborating or contradicting evidence, testability using the scientific method, compliance with natural law, attendance to Occam's Razor, and scrutiny given vast amounts of data gleaned from voluminous readings of masters of the hard scientific disciplines, social sciences, history, philosophy and comparative religion. I take nothing on blind faith.

Inquisitor: "As to Charge Number Three: *'having everything figured out'*, how does the defendant camel plead?"

Hump: "<u>Not Guilty</u>, Oh Servant of Mass Delusion."

Only religionists retain an unerring hold on their belief system, unchanged since its inception. It is *they* who claim to have it all "*figured out.*" The Free Thinker knows that real knowledge evolves, is

refined, is improved upon through more investigation, information and better technology. Things we
don't know we say we don't know. We do not fear our
current level of understanding to be shown to be
lacking, nor do we fear seeing it revised with better
information and evidence – we eagerly look forward
to it.

Inquisitor: "As to Charge Number Four: *'rejecting a
relationship with Jesus, & using Secular Books to Expand
your Knowledge Beyond the Things of The Kingdom'*, how
does the defendant camel plead?"

Hump: "<u>Guilty,</u> Your Eminence of Ignorance."

I confess my brain lacks the need to delude itself
into acceptance of the currently prevailing, or any,
god myths. My brain is free from the need to pretend
that something supernatural requires my belief, and
will reward me with life after death for it, or conversely
will punish me for not buying in. I reject it entirely as
self-imposed subservience to age old ignorance. I admit to expanding my knowledge of the natural world,
the only world that can be shown to exist. Yes, I reject
as nonsense the "great beyond," "The Kingdom," "the
Here After," or any other euphemisms for Valhalla, the
Underworld, Heaven, Hell, Hades, et al.

As of this writing the jury is still out. But given the
fact that fanatical Christians still walk among us, refusing to read secular books and carrying the mentality of
the Dark Ages with them, I fully anticipate a verdict of
BLASPHEMY!   I welcome it.

14

Why Man Exists: Mystery Solved

10 Feb 2008

The whole premise of a "why" to Man's existence, *"What is the purpose of life?"* is strictly a philosophical and theistic proposition. One may as well ask *"How many angels can dance on the head of a pin?"* It has no scientific basis, thus does not lend itself to be tested or falsified, etc. It falls in the domain of mental masturbation, practiced most especially among those who refute the scientific theories and evidence for the origin and development of life, aka theists.

Suppose we were to ask: *"Why does the AIDS virus exist?"* Scientists will say because it was a genetic mutation of another life form, and give details on its geographic origins and how it's transmitted, etc. There is neither a philosophical question of *"Why…for what purpose?"* nor an attempt to answer it. Its cause (if known) is the only why, a material answer. Anything else falls into the domain of the philosophical or theist netherworld.

Many Christians will reply that AIDS is a result of Adam and Eve's fall from grace, and thus punishment for (or fruits of) original sin. Fundies take it one obscene step further and declare AIDS a very special punishment for those who defy God's law, homosexuals. For Christians the "causal why" isn't even a first consideration or any consideration at all. How it formed, its root cause and properties are unimportant to them. The esoteric, religionist's "purposeful why" is all they can conceive.

If we ask: *"Why do stars exist?"* Astronomers and physicists will likely give you the theories of origin of the Universe, composition, energy, mass, life span, etc. The fundie will say something biblically inane such as *"To give man light by which to see at night,"* or *"God has His reasons."* It appears to be a limitation in the thinking ability of religiously impaired people whose scientific curiosity is suppressed, and whose "why" is limited to purpose. But common to all their answers is the imagined unique relationship between Mankind and the Universe as a whole. Even stars are there for Man's benefit. It's all about Man.

So why do theists have this peculiar focus on Man's Purpose, the meaning of life, and the purposefulness of everything in relation to humans? Because they are taught to be egocentric, species-centric and "Earth-centric" by their scripture. They are taught that humans are more important, thus more purposeful, than everything else in the universe. They cannot, after years of religious mind rinsing, comprehend that Man has no exclusive purposeful significance or importance. In that infinite vastness of the universe human existence doesn't even register as a sub-microscopic particle, no more so than does a grain of sand on a beach, a rock floating past Alpha Centauri, the rings of Saturn, or the yet-to-be-discovered life forms existing somewhere among the billions of suns, with billions of planets, hundreds of millions of light years away.

So here, theists, are the answers to your quest: The purpose of ones life is what one makes of his life. Species wide, the purpose of life is to perpetuate the human race, just as propagating the species is the purpose of every life form. The why of our existence is attributable to cosmic dust and the forces of nature, just as they likely happened in other worlds yet to be discovered.

Deal with it.

15

The Bleating of the Sheep: A Primer on Christian Platitudes

18 Feb 2008

Platitude: A trite or banal remark or statement, especially one expressed as if it were original or significant. See Synonyms for <u>cliché</u>.

A trademark of the most vapid believers is the hackneyed phrases they use to express their credulity and devotion. We've all seen them: The one-liners that unintentionally expose the user as possessing all the intellect and originality of the ewe or ram with which they identify.

My favorites are the ones sprinkled with biblical language like "thou," "thee," and "ye." They imagine it makes them sound more apostle-like, like some biblical figure. They equate antiquated verbiage with a higher degree of holiness, not realizing they are mimicking the syntax and speech common to the Elizabethan and post Elizabethan Age of the King James era. It's always a hoot.

Having witnessed, or been on the receiving end of countless Christian platitudes, I have become something of a connoisseur. As such, I have classified them into four main categories and provided some of my favorite Christian inanities.

I. Pious Platitudes:

Used with fellow believers, it's the sheep's version of sanctimonious one-upmanship, offered as proof that their devotion and relationship with God is more than just skin deep. Examples:

"God is bigger than my natural eyes can see." [versus "unnatural" eyes??]

"You have encouraged my faith in God."

"Jesus just loves and receives me As- is ... Right now ... Period."

"When we try to write God off as an emotional response, He still pursues us." (Yep ... it's called the "religious meme.")

II. Playbook Platitudes:

When faced with social situations that call for pat one-liners, as when attempting to comfort a deceased believer's family, or stupidly mumbled to non-believers out of ignorance. Examples:

"Don't be sad, Little Timmy is with Jesus now."

"Just trust God."

"God called little Bobby home."

"Little Susie is in our prayers."

"She's in a better place now."

"Jesus holds you in His loving arms during your hour of grief."

"I'll offer blessings of comfort and strength."

"I'll pray for you."

III. Proselytizing Platitudes:

Used in discourse (I use that word generously here) with non-believers, to attempt to divert attention from their failure to deal head on with the tough challenges; or to try and induce instant conversion to their delusion. Examples:

"Just open your heart to Jesus." (also known as the "Stop Thinking!!" gambit)

"The proof of Him is all around you."

"Jesus is my personal Lord and Savior let Him be yours as well."

"He died for your sins."

"Why are you angry at God?" or *Why do you hate God??"*

"If a Christian hurt you at some time, I'm sorry."

"You deny Him with your words, but you know that He lives."

"The Lord loves you and He is quite capable to communicate that to you and to cause you to believe, whether you want to or not."

"I'll pray for you."

IV. Pissed Off Platitudes:

Any expression of disdain using secular vernacular is discouraged among the faithful. Thus phrases such as *"Screw your logic and higher IQ, you non-believing, hell-bound bastard."* would be considered bad form. Instead, they roll out some tried and true Christian phrases that they wield like a flaming sword to express their anger or frustration. Examples:

"Begone, Satan!!"

"So you know the Bible, so what?! Even Satan can quote scripture!"

"I shake the dust from my feet."

"You'll see the error of your ways when you standeth before Him and tremble!"

"Every knee shall bend … you just wait!"

"Only a fool says there is no God! Thou art a Fool!!"

"If you don't believe in God and Heaven, why don't you just kill yourself!?"

"I'll enjoy watching you burn in Hell for eternity."

"I'll pray for you."

And on they go the bleating of minds drained of reason replaced with slavish superstition. Fine, you pray for me, or kill a chicken, or sacrifice a virgin … and I'll think for you.

16

Christian Revisionism: Ignorance or Agenda?

22 Feb 2008

Once a week stuffed in my mail box is a copy of *The Shopper News,* our free local goods and services advertising newspaper. I typically never read them. But during lunch I was leafing through the week's edition when I came across a thousand word (!!) letter to the editor.

In it, a clearly under-educated Christian went on and on about this being a "Christian Nation." How the Founding Fathers were all men of Christ. How scripture can easily be seen in the Constitution, etc. All bald-faced invention of the Christian revisionists. Naturally I couldn't let this just slide by unchallenged.

The following is my letter to the editor in response. It was published in the next issue. Feel free to use it should you observe similar theist distortion of historical fact.

Dear Sir or Madam:

Until today my wife and I were happy to have your publication delivered to our home. We regularly patronize many of your advertisers. But after reading today's edition, with its rather lengthy letter to the editor from a religious fanatic, we are having second thoughts. I object to having a publication delivered to my home, without my consent, that gives a platform for this kind of misinformation, blatant distortions, and religious zealotry.

I won't go into great detail explaining the absurdities, and lack of knowledge of US history that pervades the revisionist's letter.

> *Nor will I expound on the extensive private writings of a number of Founding Fathers, whose contempt for Christianity is widely published and easily confirmed (Jefferson and Madison being among the most vehement in their expressions).*

> *Nor shall I point out that the Constitution is devoid of any reference to God, gods, Jesus, any supernaturalism or Biblical scripture.*

> *Nor will I bother to detail Jefferson's letter of Jan. 1, 1802 describing the intent and purpose of the First Amendment's Establishment Clause as specifically creating "a wall of separation between church and state."*

> *Nor shall I copy and paste here the entire Treaty of Tripoli (1796), ratified by the Senate and signed by President John Adams in 1797, which plainly stated that "... the United States is not a Christian nation."*

> *Nor shall I bother to quote Jefferson who, in a letter dated February 10, 1814 stated that the Common Law,*

*the foundation for the Constitution, as drawn from
English law, has no basis in Christianity.*

*No ... I won't do any of that. Any moderately-educated
student of history willing to suspend their personal agenda,
willing to disassociate their personal "beliefs" from the public
facts, can discover this for themselves.*

*That Christians played an important role (along with
Jews, Deists, and atheists) in the development of our country
is not at issue here. Neither is the fact that some/ many of the
Founders prayed or read the Bible. It's all good. What's at
issue is your suborning ignorance, misinformation and the
need for some people to promulgate the erroneous belief that
this country favors their religion over another religion or over
no religion at all. Please stop it, or stop putting your publication in my mailbox.*

Thank you.

17

Which is the True Religion of Peace?

28 Feb 2008

Islam likes to refer to itself as the *Religion of Peace.* It doesn't take a rocket scientist to figure out that the "peace" they offer isn't for apostates, infidels, "People of the Book" (aka Christians and Jews), Hindus, or Buddhists. The thousands of terrorist acts of murder and destruction perpetrated in the name of the prophet Mohammed over the past thirty-five years makes that clear. At best the peace Islam professes to offer is only for their adherents ... and not necessarily female adherents, but that's a matter of interpretation and cultural perspective.

Naturally, it takes some mental gymnastics to figure out how Middle East Muslim countries and Islamic radical political parties indoctrinate elementary school children with hate, teach them arms, and instill a willingness to kill and die, and still call that *"peaceful."* Nor is it easy for the Western mind to reconcile peace with strapping bombs onto two Down Syndrome Muslim women and remotely detonating them in a crowded market place. I guess the simple answer is they find peace in death. Wonderful! Add to that the riots and deaths due to Muslim furor over those Danish cartoons of their prophet. As for their scripture, the Koran is rife with references to killing in the name of Allah, too many to be dismissed simply as problems of context.

So, if Islam isn't the religion of peace, which religion truly deserves the vaunted title? Well, the Jews never were in the running. A cursory perusal of the Old Testament with its numerous horrendous acts of murder, rape, infanticide, genocide and enslavement committed by the chosen people at the behest of their God sort of disqualifies them as peace merchants.

Of the Abrahamic religions that leaves Christianity. What can we look to in Christianity that qualifies it for the Peace title? Well, let's see.

Christian dogma is as exclusionary and intolerant as they come. The New Testament says all who don't believe like them are condemned to suffer eternal torment burning in a lake of fire in Hell. It's the ONLY religion on the planet that espouses such an intolerant, exclusive and hideously obscene point of view. Hardly a peaceful message there.

And what does that intolerance and exclusivity generate? With the Jews' rejection of Jesus as the true Messiah (the deliverer of Israel from foreign oppression as promised in the Old Testament) Paul plays the "Gentile card," and gives the prospective new Roman converts, the true killers of their man-god, a pass. Instead, he condemns the Jews as the scapegoat for their mythical man-god's demise. Presto!!! Two-thousand years of anti-Semitism is born, and with it every pogrom in Europe, every extermination attempt, every religion tax, every exile of Jews, every Jewish joke,

every exclusion of Jews from universities, every restricted country club, can all be traced back to and
laid at the feet of Christian doctrine right up through,
and including, the Holocaust. Thanks to Paul for that
peace-inducing doctrine that has never fully gone out
of style.

Then there are the Crusades, the blood bath bestowed on Jews, Coptic Christians and Muslims; the
extermination of the Cathars; the murder of the Tem-
plar's; the torture and death of the Inquisitions; the
forced conversions of native peoples; the torture and
burning of "witches" right up into the 18th century.

And on it goes into the 21st century with the exclusion, discrimination and violence toward homosexuals;
demonization of atheists as non patriots, un-American,
lacking of morals and ethics unfit to hold public office;
the call to bomb abortion clinics, to kill the doctors;
the endorsement of assassination of foreign leaders by
the most renowned televangelist; the dogma that warns
that the one who petitions for and brings peace to the
Middle East will be revealed as The Anti-Christ! You
see, bringing peace in the Middle East will stand in the
way of The End Times, Armageddon, the prophesized
end of the world, something many Christians actually
want to see happen and indeed, encourage. Christianity
a peaceful religion? I think not.

Now, moderate Christians, just like moderate Muslims, will say the evils that are done in the name of
God/Christ/Allah are perversions of their religion.
That Christ was the "Prince of Peace," even while he
clearly stated he hadn't come to bring peace (Matthew
10:34). They will tell us that the Christian zealots
who committed those horrendous acts down through
history, or who profess violence, intolerance and

hatred today pervert scripture and use it for their own purposes. They will say they are reading the Bible out of "context." That those are not "true Christians. Well, how very convenient. Seems to me their God might have seen that coming, would have made Its wishes more clear and concise eliminating any points of confusion as to His dictates and intent. After all, they claim their god is perfect and omniscient. Evidently, he sucks as an author and editor.

No, I'm afraid the title *"Religion of Peace"* has no legitimate claimant. Religion has left death, pain and misery in its wake since man invented God/gods. Indeed, the very phrase "religion of peace" is a contradiction in terms, an oxymoron – like "silent scream."

18

The Supernatural Needs No Explanation

07 Mar 2008

Many times atheists will get themselves all in a tizzy trying to explain how the supernatural can't exist, because when the physical law for a supernatural event is discovered it becomes "natural" law. But I contend that they are over-thinking this.

Theists have forever attributed natural events for which they had no explanation to God, Satan, miracles and the realm of the supernatural. Lightning strikes, two headed calves, eclipses, Black Plague, famine, drought, locusts, floods, foreign invaders, earthquakes, volcanic eruptions, epileptic seizures, you name it, at some point in pre-scientific man's history, and not very long ago, it was an indicator and omen of some god's wrath, mercy, or the workings of an evil being.

That we now know what causes these things dispels attributing them to the supernatural pretty much for everyone in the modern world. The more knowledge man attains, the fewer the default explanations of *"God/the supernatural did it"* thus, the smaller the *"God of the gaps"* explanation has become. God has gotten much smaller over the past 300 years thanks to the scientific age and discovery.

But I have never seen, nor has any theist ever shown me, a supernatural event. Therefore, the cause, the natural law necessary to explain the event, never comes into play, because there is no event/no effect, to observe and explain. Thus to attribute a non-event to some natural law is like trying to find an answer to a question never asked. [More on this subject in Chapter 40.]

As I see it there are four levels of supernatural non-events for which no natural law causal explanation is needed:

<u>Physical Manifestations:</u> The appearance of Mary on a grilled cheese sandwich, or Jesus as a bird dropping on a church window, is as close to physical supernatural evidence as theists seem to get. The fact of the latter image's composition and that it often looks as much like Willy Nelson as it does Jesus to an impartial party, pretty much negates any serious compulsion to invoke natural law to explain it.

<u>Wishful Thinking:</u> A devout Christian once told me he attributed hearing a hospital nurse singing his terminally ill relative's favorite hymn as a sign, proof of God's presence. No natural law need be presented to explain it. The fact it was a Catholic hospital replete with singing nuns, and the need for a sign by a highly receptive and distraught subject speaks for itself. But trying to get that across to the religiously impaired and willfully credulous is hardly worth the effort.

Hearsay: Jesus' resurrection, Moses parting the Red Sea, frog plague ... some people, non-theists no less, try to come up with natural cause explanations for these fables, such as strong winds parting the sea, or a water spout throwing frogs into the air, or Jesus having been in a coma. But these stories are as much evidence of actual events as *Star War's* Boba Fett is proof of inter-stellar bounty hunters, or "ET" is proof of alien visitations. How much time really need be devoted to exploring the possibility that the fictional "ET" might possibly have been a mutant possum?

Deliverance Miracles: The fiery plane crash that kills everyone on board except the infant who's thrown clear ... *"IT'S A MIRACLE!!"* Aunt Sadie's cancer goes into remission ... *"MIRACULOUS!!!"* Well, would it have been a miracle if everyone in that horrible crash survived *except* the infant child? And wouldn't it have been more miraculous had Aunt Sadie *not* undergone surgery, chemo and radiation therapy and instead depended ONLY on the miraculous healing power of God through prayer? No natural law explanation needed, since nothing supernatural has been demonstrated to require it.

So, where are these supernatural events which defy natural law and necessitate evaluation with the scientific method? When Aunt Sadie's rotting corpse drops by for tea with Jesus in tow, call me. I'll be right over with a gaggle of accredited scientists.

19

The Trinity as Proof of God

15 Mar 2008

I've heard the argument made by Christians that the concept of the Trinity is so unique to Man's experience, so outside the realm of human comprehension and understanding, that it stands as proof of God. Then reason rears its head and spoils everything.

The concept of trinity didn't originate with Christianity. It was a Hindu concept (the three personages of Brahma, Vishnu, Shiva in one God) long before Christianity. The Egyptians and ancient Greeks also had a trinity concept. The theme of trinity, albeit non-deity related, was a Platonic theme. The early Christians were aware of all this. Combine that with the fact that Christian scripture (the *"Word of God,"* don't forget) is devoid of the term Trinity, and that "three personages in one God" was ratified and adopted by the church at the Council of Constantinople in 381 C.E. by VOTE; how anyone could perceive Trinity as anything other than an early Christian invention co-opted from their Hindu, Egyptian or Greek predecessors is beyond me.

There were all kinds of doctrinal decisions and edicts made from the 4th through 8th centuries in an effort to define the qualities of Jesus, and to establish a single dogma from many prevailing views. Trinity was just one of them. Is it any more a mystery as to how Trinity was created than how a god with two faces, or one with four arms, or one that sprang from the head of another was conceived? Are any beyond the realm of human comprehension/imagination? Isn't each one of those gods outside our "experience?" And by it being so, does it make it real or true? Obviously not.

As for the Christian trinity being outside our understanding, it's on a par with any unusual and convoluted fictional concept. Do any of us understand the forces, biology, natural laws or mechanisms that allow Spiderman to climb up walls? Do we require an understanding of how Prometheus' liver regenerated each day so it could be torn out and eaten the next? Do we even bother to give it a second thought? Is it worthy of consideration? Is it evidence of the supernatural? Not if you still have possession of your ability to think rationally.

20

When Logic and Belief Collide: The Christian Dilemma

21 Mar 2008

In a friendly liberal Christian blog site a Christian working with war refugee children in Sudan posted a letter to her fellow church members. Clearly the writer is a dedicated and committed person, and is doing good works which of course she attributes to God's calling. Among the readership of that blog are many platitudinous murmuring Christians the kind who leave comments like this:

"Until the world acknowledges Sudan and gets on it knees and cries for God's mercy on this region, it will not substantially change at the hands of governments."

I am a tolerated atheist guest there and it's not a debate blog, so I'm not about to reply and play mean old logical atheist spoiler (something at least one other regular had already accused me of). So, out of respect for the blog owner I opted to withhold comment. Instead I sent the fundie's comment along with four questions to a Christian friend. Here they are:

1) If God were omniscient, omnipotent, omni-benevolent, obviously he would be aware of the conditions in Sudan. He would have the power to do something about it, and with His divine benevolence He wouldn't need to be begged for "mercy" to respond. He would do the right thing independent of pleas. *So, why is prayer needed, and why doesn't he do the right thing proactively, without prompting?*

2) Since worldwide prayers are a prerequisite to get God's attention, it infers that prayer volume is the critical element necessary to resolve Sudan's problems. It presupposes that God reacts to and prioritizes his responses based on the number and/or intensity of prayers. *So, if one person's prayers aren't sufficient to provoke God's action, how many does it take for prayer to be generally effective?* 72 people? 123,000 people? 3 million people? All 6.7 billion people on the planet?

3) Christians always tout that God gives man "free will," and thus does not intervene and influence man's thinking by manipulating his brain. If this is basic doctrine then the prayers for God's mercy must be asking for God's direct, divine, and miraculous intervention in Sudan. *Why is the fundie expecting God to effect a substantial change through governmental (Man's) action, unless he doesn't believe in free will or he's asking God to violate the free will doctrine?*

4) Finally, when was the last time civil strife and war was directly stayed by God's direct divine intervention and not by the intervention of a military force or threat of same? *Remembering that with "free will" God would not force men's minds to form a saving force. As far as a force of arms, God would be limited to an army of His personal heavenly host.*

Unfortunately, my Christian friend demurred and opted out instead offering that any answer she could supply would never satisfy my purely logical thinking process. She also inferred I was intent on ridiculing her beliefs (irrefutable reasoning does have a way of sounding condescending to theists, I suppose). But I surmise that what was really happening was that inescapable dilemma theists have wrestled with for years: The rational part of the brain whispers *"reason...logic!"* but the religion meme shouts *"Stop That!!"*

21

Happy Easter aka Resurrection of Mithras Day

22 Mar 2008

Mythology tells us that the god Mithras was born to the virgin Anahita in a cave, on December 25th. With twelve disciples Mithras travelled far and wide as a teacher and illuminator of men. At about age 30 he began his ministry, offering salvation based on faith, compassion, knowledge and valor.

Suffering a violent death, Mithras arose from his tomb, an event celebrated annually at the Spring equinox. After the earthly mission of this god had been accomplished, he took part in a last supper with his companions before ascending to paradise, to forever protect the faithful from above.

The similarities to Christianity go on in much more detail including his baptism, and his having atoned for all man's sins. Coincidence? Did the followers of Mithras co-opt their god fable from Jesus and the Christian tradition? Not likely, since the cult of Mithras preceded Christianity by more than six-hundred years.

In fact there are numerous pagan gods whose virgin or unusual births, violent deaths and subsequent resurrections and elevation into paradise are common themes.[1]

How do Christians deal with this? One of two ways. They either deny such a god figure existed, out of ignorance or avoidance; or like the famous 2nd century Christian apologist Justin Martyr (1 Apologia, 66, 4), they denounce the devil for having sent a God so similar to Jesus – *yet preceding him*.

As Christians celebrate their Easter, they are in fact celebrating the Resurrection Festival of Mithras, and of course the Spring equinox. His will be done.

---

[1] http://www.wilsonsalmanac.com/jesus_similar.html

22

Why Christians Lie

29 Mar 2008

Whether its claiming prayer cured them from AIDS, or spontaneously healed their severed spinal column; or swearing they have spoken to Jesus, or seen angels, or Satan (pick one or more); or distorting scientific proofs by inventing inaccurate characterizations (i.e. "Evolution says men came from monkeys"; "many scientists believe in Intelligent Design"), it appears theists just have a problem with honesty.

While some of it may be attributable to hyper-religiosity (an accepted clinical term associated with schizophrenia) or just plain stupidity, there seems to be a propensity toward intentional deception. My studied opinion is that when a theistic assertion cannot be supported by evidence, or when they are faced with the overwhelming evidence of scientific theory, or the logic of a rational mind, Christians have nothing left except distortion with which to defend their position and belief. They lie out of desperation to protect their faith. It's virtually a reflex.

But how can lying be sanctioned in a belief system that claims a higher morality than non-belief and bases its entire philosophy on "Truth?" Because lying is sanctioned by their church Fathers. More than one eminent theist has endorsed lying to promulgate the faith:

"How it may be Lawful and Fitting to use Falsehood as a Medicine, and for the Benefit of those who Want to be Deceived."
 – Bishop Eusebius, 4th century Christian scholar

"Do you see the advantage of deceit?
... For great is the value of deceit, provided it be not introduced with a mischievous intention. In fact action of this kind ought not to be called deceit, but rather a kind of good management, cleverness and skill, capable of finding out ways where resources fail, and making up for the defects of the mind
... And often it is necessary to deceive, and to do the greatest benefits by means of this device, whereas he who has gone by a straight course has done great mischief to the person whom he has not deceived."
 – John Chrysostom, 5th century theologian, Treatise On The Priesthood, Book 1

"We should always be disposed to believe that which appears to us to be white is really black, if the hierarchy of the church so decides."
 – Ignatius Loyola, 16th century founder of the Jesuits

And finally this:

"What harm would it do, if a man told a good strong lie for the sake of the good and for the Christian church ... a lie out of necessity, a useful lie, a helpful lie, such lies would not be against God, he would accept them."

– Martin Luther, 16th century theologian, Christian reformer, founder of Lutheranism.

Add to these endorsements of deception the notorious forgeries of scriptural support documents, intentional translational distortions of the Hebrew bible to justify Christian doctrine, textual interpolation, and the re-writing of history by Christian apologists, and lying is clearly not only very Christian, it's a veritable sacrament.

23

"Context!" The Last Refuge of a Theist in Denial

01 Apr 2008

Whether it's trying to defend the hideous malevolent acts of cruelty, genocide and murder by their loving Old Testament God; fumbling to counter biblical contradictions; or trying to justify why their Omni-benevolent being failed to condemn slavery or why Jesus kills perfectly good fig trees, Christians invariably will deny all and cry *"Context!!"*

"Context!!" has become the trademark of Christians who are at a loss to explain away the indefensible cruelties performed by their perfect, loving God, or used to make the embarrassing statements of their saintly Church figures go away. Context has become so overused that it typically triggers laughter among Thinking People [TP] who have seen it employed so often that it is now a cliché. Here's how it works:

TP: "According to OT law, God demands that a woman's hand be cut off if she intervenes with her husband's attacker and grabs his genitals." (Deut. 25:11-12)

Christian: *"OH ... you're taking it out of context."*

TP: "Forty-two children misbehave, show disrespect, are cursed by a prophet and God sends bears to tear them apart." (2 Kings 2:23-24)

Christian: *"OH ... you're taking it out of context."*

TP: "God commanded every inhabitant of a tribe to be destroyed, every animal, and just the virgin women to be kidnapped and kept by the Hebrews as breeding stock. There are numerous examples of God suborning genocide and rape."

Christian: *"OH ... you're talking it out of context."*

Ok. So what I need to hear and yet never do is the answer to this question: In what *"context"* is killing children for their words, lopping off a woman's defending hand, extermination of a civilization and the enslavement and rape of virgins justifiable by any supremely merciful being at anytime? Just tell me in what *"context"* I should be reading that scripture to make it all sane, just and good?

But, they can't. Call their bluff and they fold. Oh, some will offer an unsupportable attempt at perversion of verse to make it seem like a good and wholly wonderful thing. Failing that they will just out right reinvent meaning for scripture: *"Well, yes... but... never mind what it actually says...here's what I say it really means."* But they are being intellectually dishonest, or deceiving themselves as usual. We know how that works, the Muslims do it with the indefensible obscenities of the Koran all the time.

Four hundred years ago, questioning the Bible could result in excommunication, torture and/or execution (Christians like to refer to those as 'The Good

Old Days"). But here in the West those things are pretty much gone. The door is open for Christians to take a deep breath, screw up their courage and exhibit a modicum of intellectual honesty and reason and say: *"Golly! You're right!! That IS a messed up thing that the Biblical authors attributed to God. I wonder why they did that, what motivated them."*

But it never gets to that. They usually can't handle that bit of unabashed honesty because once that happens, once that door is cracked open, once doubt as to the veracity of "God's Word" comes into play their entire foundation of faith is subject to reexamination/rethinking. No! Better to hold the line, ignore the obvious, and like the emperor with no clothes, cling to some transparent ploy to cover the nakedness of their inane book of fable and blind belief and just dumbly cry *"CONTEXT!!"*

24

Perverting History: Christian Deception Personified

05 Apr 2008

On a Catholic apologetics site, they tell their faithful how the Inquisitions were not really as bad as people think. Oh yes, there were some excesses to be sure, but not nearly as horrible as some would have you believe. Here's the passage:

"There have actually been several different inquisitions. The first was established in 1184 in southern France as a response to the Cathar heresy. This was known as the Medieval Inquisition, **and it was phased out as Catharism disappeared."** [1]

"... *Phased out as Catharism disappeared?!?*" Yeah, I'll say!! The little detail the good Catholic apologists fail to mention is that Catharism *"disappeared"* not by the choice of the Cathars, but thanks to the Catholic Church's twenty-year genocidal Albigensian Crusade, which virtually wiped out all the Cathars, men, women and children. Yes, they are right, the complete and

---

[1] http://www.catholic.com/library/inquisition.asp

utter destruction of an alternate religion by the Church will indeed cause the Inquisition to *"phase out."* [2]

Using this logic, this example of revisionist history and Christian truth telling, let's apply it to the 19th century Indian Wars here in the US. The Army's explanation would read something like this: *"The campaign against the Indians by the US Army during the 19th Century lasted some twenty-five years. It was in response to the Native American's failure to acquiesce to the White Man's demands and quietly allow their culture to be destroyed. This was known as the Indian Wars, **and was phased out as the American Indian disappeared."***

Makes perfect sense if you're attempting to sugar coat an abhorrent past, replete with persecution and genocide. Historical revisionism and perversion of truth, thy name is Christianity.

25
Christian Psychosis: Doing the Lord's Evil
09 Apr 2008

The other night as I was watching the local news, a report came on about a beloved elder Christian minister, a high ranking church official, who was caught in a church van raping a 15- year-old boy, a member of his congregation. Twenty-five years ago this would be big news and cause uproar. Today clergy abuse is so commonplace that it's met with *"So, what else is new?"* barely raising eyebrows.

Earlier in the week there was another report about the polygamist Fundamentalist Mormons, whose leader, Warren Jeffs, is in prison for suborning the rape of a 14-year-old sect member and other children. Authorities were initially refused access to their temple to search for a 16-year-old mother (and wife to a 50-year-old man) who had called police for help. The girl has yet to be located, although 200 women and children were removed from the "compound."

Over the past three weeks there have been two separate and well-publicized cases of parents of Christian sects refusing to seek medical help for their children (one with diabetes and the other with pneumonia). While they prayed to God for their children's recovery, both died agonizing deaths. Medical experts said the children could have been saved by timely medical treatment.

About once a year we hear about a Christian mother killing her children because she was directed to do so by God; or because she wanted them to have a better existence in heaven; or as a result of administering extreme corporal punishment where the "Good Book" was invoked as a guide and justification.

I'm not suggesting that rape, polygamy, child abuse and child murder is the sole provenance of Christianity. But clearly these acts, especially the three latter examples, are directly influenced by devotion to the supernatural, indoctrination by religious leaders, and influence of religious scripture. Surely without the concepts of God, Heaven, Hell, Satan, salvation, "God's Will," damnation, etc., being implanted in their minds in early childhood these horrific events would never have occurred. These are anti-social/psychotic acts that are directly related to their faith and belief system which they claim is the "one true way." That's what makes these acts particularly grotesque.

One thing I know for sure, you'll never hear about a confirmed atheist raping a child and convincing them its okay because it is "Darwin's Will," and intimidating him/her with the **absence** of hellfire and damnation for reporting the abuse.

I know of no atheist organizations, or atheist "cults," which suborn polygamy, child marriage and statutory rape, much less invoke interpretations of writings by

Dawkins, Hitchens, Robert Price, Sam Harris or Mark Twain as justification for same.

I can find no example where atheist parents stood over their sick child chanting from a copy of *"The Portable Atheist"* or *"Origin of Species,"* withheld professional medical attention and watched their child convulsed with fever die in the throes of agony.

I'm unaware of any atheist mother dismembering and murdering her children because they were compelled to do so by the spirits or voices of Carl Sagan, Ernest Hemingway, or Kurt Vonnegut; or because they were convinced that the rotting non-existence of the grave was better for their child than a full and healthy life.

It prompts the questions: Are Christians drawn to Christianity/religiosity because they are despicable perverts, utterly insane, or patently stupid? Or are they driven to psychotic behavior as a result of their religious belief?

26

Jesus: Real or Fiction & Does it Make a Difference?

13 Apr 2008

In Galatians 1:19 Paul writes of having met Jesus' brother, James. Some Christians claim this is evidence that Jesus was a real person, although there are no legitimate contemporary eyewitness accounts corroborating a real Jesus outside of the bible.

That Paul writes he hobnobbed with James is somehow taken as a confirmation that Jesus was real. Talk about a leap of faith. Paul also said he met with Jesus after his death. Paul said the laws of the Hebrew Bible were now null and void, although Jesus said they never would be until the Earth disappeared and "all was accomplished." Paul said women shouldn't preach in church and that rulers never do evil to the innocent. Paul said a lot of shit. So, how does anything Paul say have any bearing on a genuine Jesus?

But, lets presuppose some character named Jesus did exist (it was among the most popular names in that region at the time, tantamount to "Bob" these days).

What is the implication and significance? That some executed Jew among thousands of executed Jews; some itinerant Cynic preacher; some hysterical mad man ala the Jesus described in Josephus' "Jewish Wars;" or some wanna be leader of a new/reformed Jewish sect, actually lived?

And that upon this individual's demise Paul and his fellow cultists borrowed from innumerable known pagan myths and conveniently revised Jewish prophesy to endow him with a divine lineage and supernatural abilities "far beyond those of mortal men?" Okay.

I don't see what possible difference it makes if Jesus was a fictional being, or some poor deluded putz who, unbeknownst to him, became the center of a cult's devotion after his death. After all, Haili Selassie, Emperor of Ethiopia, existed, is deemed God, and is worshipped to this day as the true savior by his devoted Rastafarian followers. Of course, Selassie was black, didn't have the right PR guys like Jesus did, and was a 20th century figure, so his post-death cult's popularity never quite caught on. [On the upside they smoke ganja as a sacrament which is eminently more attractive than dried out wafers and watered down wine or grape Kool Aid.]

So, my questions are simple: What "evidence" is there of a real Jesus? And what difference does it make?

27

Pope-O-Mania: Rose Petals for a Tyrant

16 Apr 2008

The visit of Pope Benedict to the US has the Catholic faithful all in a tizzy. I imagine they are sweeping out their churches, getting their Sunday best dry cleaned, polishing their crucifixes and hiding their pre-teen sons and daughters in anticipation of this "historic event," as it has been dubbed by the news media.

Given this man's credentials, and the philosophy he represents, they should stop him at the airport, conduct a body cavity search, and then have him immediately deported like any other unsavory character. Harsh? Maybe. But what exactly makes his visit more "historic" and of more importance than a visit by any backward-thinking ruler of a totalitarian city-state, or high ranking witch doctor from some prehistoric animist culture? More succinctly, what exactly does the office of Pope stand for or contribute to society? What has he accomplished that justifies the adoration, anticipation and intense media coverage?

Vatican City produces nothing. It neither sows nor reaps. It produces no commodity or natural resource. It hasn't advanced medicine, or developed new technology to improve the human condition or benefit mankind. And yet, while it claims to be cash poor, it accumulated vast wealth and property much of it from contributions extorted from those who can least afford it.

It has virtually no political influence, nor does it have the force of power to intercede in armed international conflicts. Its leadership is appointed in secret by a closed hierarchy, not democratically elected by those over whom it seeks to wield power. This Pope was a member of the Hitler Youth movement. In the past he repeated an unthinking, politically charged comment that enflamed the Muslim world.

Catholic dogma against condoms has contributed to the spread of AIDS, as well as overpopulation, and thus has propagated hunger and a lower standard of living in many Third World countries. For decades it has actively engaged in a coordinated cover-up of sexual misconduct by its emissaries, often depicting the violators as the victims and the victims as the perpetrators.

The legacy of the Church is fraught with innumerable horrors: The destruction of cultures and murder of indigenous peoples; the torture and genocide of those who don't accept its doctrine; instigation and suborning of war to amass wealth; the persecution of "witches" driven by ignorant superstition; a lineage of leadership who count among their number murderers, rapists, fornicators, Nazi sympathizers and anti-Semites; the subjugation of women and persecution of homosexuals; the suppression of knowledge and scientific inquiry, often by threat of imprisonment, torture and death.

And all this in the name of some un-seeable, unprovable, imaginary Sky Daddy.

So they roll out the red carpet, trumpet his arrival, fill Yankee Stadium, shout the hosannas, kiss his ring, wave the handkerchiefs, hold up their babies for a blessing, and swoon at the pageantry and the glittering costumes. I can hardly wait for the movie to come out. Maybe they can call it *"The Triumph of the Will II."*

28

Test Your Knowledge, Name This Jew Hater

19 Apr 2008

Anti-Semitism is nothing new. It's been around almost 2000 years, ever since Jews rejected Jesus as a false messiah. When they did that, Paul, seeing a dead end for the cult, decided that making Jews the scapegoat for Jesus' death was the perfect way to exonerate the Romans, and thus draw them, the gentiles, into what Jesus had intended to be a reformed Jewish movement. Voila!! 2000 years of anti-Semitism was born.

There have been a lot of Jew haters. Many use the words of the New Testament to justify hating and persecuting Jews. Their hate can be subtle or vehement. It can manifest itself as simple exclusion of Jews, spreading hateful stereotypes and falsehoods, or physical violence against them. Some hardcore anti-Semites became world famous for fanning the fires of hate, dehumanizing Jews and infecting others with their intolerance, prompting widespread and intense Jewish persecution.

The following are the words of a famous Jew hater. A man whose name is renowned the world over, with a following of millions. Can you name him?

> ➤ He argued that the Jews were no longer the chosen people, but were *"the devil's people."*

> ➤ He wrote that Jews were *"base, whoring people, that is, no people of God, and their boast of lineage, circumcision, and law must be accounted as filth."*

> ➤ The synagogue was a *"defiled bride, yes, an incorrigible whore and an evil slut ..."* – Jews were full of the *"devil's feces ... which they wallow in like swine."*

> ➤ He advocated setting synagogues on fire, destroying Jewish prayer books, forbidding rabbis from preaching, seizing Jewish property and money, smashing up their homes and ensuring that these *"poisonous envenomed worms"* be forced into labor or *"expelled for all time."*

> ➤ He also sanctioned their murder, writing *"We are at fault in not slaying them."*

So, who do you think it was?   Hitler? Goebbels? American Nazi Party leader George Lincoln Rockwell? An infamous atheist? Stalin? Marx? Trotsky? Some rabid Islamic imam? The President of Iran? Osama bin Laden? No. It was a man of God, a paragon of Christian values, a dedicated monk, a reformer and the founder of Lutheranism, Martin Luther.

Surprised? You shouldn't be. Without the hate and intolerance wrought by Christian scripture and its devout followers, anti-Semitism would have never existed. Christians were and remain the keepers of the flame.

29

Christian Charity: Altruism with an Agenda

23 Apr 2008

A Christian woman I know from the internet is pretty cool. Not fanatical, belongs to a very liberal church, she has no problem with my atheism. She enthusiastically touts the good works of her mega church in which she is very active and proud. Her church has adopted a village in Africa. Each year members volunteer to go, at their own expense, to help improve the infrastructure, assist with teaching, provide books, increase food production, etc.

Next fall my Christian friend and her husband are going to Africa. She is trying to raise money via her blog to help finance their travel costs. I was initially a tad ambivalent. From my knowledge of Christian charitable organizations, like various "12 step programs," "faith-based" government funded organizations, the Salvation Army, even relief efforts in Southeast Asia after the 2004 tsunami, all of them placed religious participation at the forefront, if not making it a pre-requisite for aiding those in need.

So I asked if this trip is fully dedicated to material/secular health, welfare, and education – life improvements for the community without any preaching, proselytizing or bible study; with no expectation of conversion from whatever indigenous belief system those people may hold. I wanted assurance that not a dime of my contribution would be spent on proselytizing or spreading "the Word." She explained that the local village church with whom they partner is the spiritual provider. Her and her husband's presence will be dedicated solely to hands on improving of the physical condition and secular life of the people. I accept her at her word and will make a donation to her and her husband's travel fund.

But other seemingly altruistic Christian charities have an ulterior motive – conversion. They dangle the carrot in front of struggling Third World people who, in a weakened state, desperate for any support, would pay any price, including abandoning their culture, in order to better their physical condition and those of their children. Is that what Jesus meant by ministering to the poor?

I don't recall Jesus saying: *"For I was hungry and you gave me food, I was thirsty and you gave me drink … and all I had to do was listen to your religious spiel and divest myself of my 3000 year old culturally-held indigenous belief system."* But that's exactly what many of them do.

That's what often passes for "Christian Charity." It's altruism, on THEIR terms, with a hook and an agenda. It seems to me that true altruism is its own reward. That to show humanity toward your fellow man and then thrust a condition upon it, either stated or implicit, cheapens the act. It defiles the very concept of charity and good will.

Today my wife and I donated groceries to the local food bank we actively support. You know what we expect in return? That fewer people go hungry. Period.

30

It Takes a Christian's Mind to Call This "God's Gift"

30 Apr 2008

I was browsing internet theist sites looking for some debate when I stumbled across this in a Christian message group. It was in reference to a newspaper report of an 11-year- old girl who was raped and then buried alive:

"God was sacrificing this child as a way to show others the light. Much as he did his own child. What a beautiful gift he has given us."

What's interesting about this statement, as sick and twisted as it is, is that the writer has done no more than any other Christian apologist who seeks to provide an excuse or justification for their mythical god's apparent unconcern/non-responsiveness to extreme evil and aberrant human behavior, or God's outright endorsement of extinguishing human life with pain and agony.

This Christian simply took the horrendous inexplicable act of a psychotic killer pedophile and imbued it with religious significance that put a happy God face on it. Praise Jesus!!!

The (happily) deceased Jerry Falwell did it with Katrina, declaring it God's wrath for New Orleans' evil ways; and by declaring the deaths of millions from AIDs as Gods vengeance. Pat Robertson did it by attributing the 3,000 innocent deaths of 9/11 to God's retribution for America's tolerance of homosexuality. They both did it, as did Muslim imams, when the 2004 tsunami killed thousands in Southeast Asia. Heck, Fred Phelps credits God with wantonly killing folks in retribution for homosexuality; it's *"God's gift"* to America he'll tell you.

If in their sick superstitious minds their God will kill thousands by permitting, even causing, terrorist attacks, hurricanes and earthquakes, then why be shocked at one more hyper-religious fundie whackjob seeing God's will in the rape and murder of one small child, and throwing a positive spin on it to boot? Besides, don't Christians put a positive spin on the death of children all the time with their platitudinous *"She's in a better place"* or *"God had a better need for her"* drivel? Isn't it in keeping with the concept of "God's Plan" which theists claim man can never really know or understand?

To hyper religious fanatics' convoluted mind gymnastics, bizarre "leaps of faith" in lieu of reason, logic, common sense, good taste and sanity are necessary to retain and justify their belief. Without this kind of obscene twisted illogic and self delusion they would be forced to see how patently absurd their total immersion in supernaturalism is, what a fraud they have bought into.

The human mind is a marvelous thing. That it can be so badly abused by the religious brain virus is pretty damn scary.

31

Refuting the Resurrection Myth & Dying for a Lie

03 May 2008

In a message group a fellow atheist sought aid in refuting a Christian's statement. It speaks to two common theist ploys: Proving you can't refute the resurrection myth, and their positing a gross misstatement as fact. Here's his posting:

"I am having a discussion on the resurrection of Jesus and the gentleman's line of reasoning goes something like this – *Jesus' disciples went to their deaths proclaiming that He did physically rise from the dead. While others may die for their faith, these first followers of Jesus knew the truth—one way or the other. I know of no example of people dying for a lie.'* Now, the last point is an argument from personal ignorance. But I was hoping to find some reference to refute the argument of the disciples' personal "knowledge" of his resurrection. Can someone point me to a good argument?"

Here's my response:

You won't find any contradicting New Testament scripture as to his disciples' belief in resurrection, if by disciples you mean the remaining eleven Apostles. And why would you? The New Testament wasn't exactly an even-handed treatment of the various perspectives of early Christians. The official canon established exactly what the church fathers wanted it to, the Jesus resurrection fable being central to the preferred Christian doctrine, as rebirth was for so many preceding pagan god myths. Dissenting interpretations were not welcome.

James (alleged brother of Jesus) was the leader of the Christian Jews who practiced a reformed Judaism, and viewed Jesus as Prophet and Rabbi, but not a deity. Thus, it is likely they did not believe in resurrection. But their take isn't admitted into church canon. The losing point of view would be suppressed, purged, redacted/revised into obscurity, leaving only 100% concurrence with the dominant cult's resurrection doctrine. In fact, in the Acts of Apostles, James' name isn't even mentioned after the year 60 CE.

According to John (20:19-23), Jesus appeared to the apostles after his death and showed them his crucifixion wounds. Thus, scripture would have you believe they all would have had "personal knowledge" that he died and was resurrected.

Now what? Trying to refute a fool's fable is a fool's errand at worst, an exercise in futility at best. You might as well try and refute Wicca theology that goddesses and gods are able to manifest in personal form; or argue with Muslims that Mohammed didn't really fly up to Paradise on his horse like the Koran says; or tell a Mormon that the Angel Moroni was a fabrication. It goes nowhere.

As for the inane comment about *"... not knowing of anyone who has ever died for a lie,"* Oscar Wilde said it best: *"A thing is not necessarily true because a man dies for it."* I'm sure you can dispatch that fallacious theist idiocy rather easily. Start with every Muslim terrorist who ever blew himself up for Allah; or every American soldier who died in Vietnam to stop the spread of Communism; or every soldier who died in Iraq, and those that will.

32

National Day of Prayer:
A National Day of Idiocy

06 May 2008

In the 1950's a lot of crazy religious proclamations were made by Congress. They added the *"Under God"* phrase to the pledge; added *"In God We Trust"* to paper currency; and declared the first Thursday in May a National Day of Prayer".

A lot of this stemmed from the Red Scare, the hysteria over the spread of Communism with Senator Joe McCarthy as the poster boy for fear, persecution and paranoia. The logic behind this sudden religiosity was based on the moronic belief that Communists wouldn't handle money, or say the pledge, or participate in prayer, thus exposing them as the godless, heathen, freedom-hating fiends that they were. A brilliant plan devised by our mostly Christian leadership.

So last Thursday theists of all sects, denominations and cults were supposed to bow their heads, or kneel, or prostrate themselves while mumbling some prayers to their respective concepts of God or gods. The focus was supposed to be prayer for our nation.

There is an official National Day of Prayer website that I will say, right here, and right now, is the shallowest, most insipid, and idiotic website I have visited since the last time I checked up on our good God-fearing Christian friend Fred Phelps. Check it out at your convenience, you won't be disappointed. http://www.ndptf.org/home/home.html

The whole website reads like a caricature of theistic stupidity at its worst. I checked twice to make sure it wasn't some parody site created by a smartass atheist. It isn't. There you will find the official prayer, a meaningless and childlike assemblage of self-serving drivel. A quick read, it infers God blesses America because it is more worthy than those other starving and hideously suffering peoples of underdeveloped nations that presumably don't HAVE a National Day of Prayer. One is left to assume those countries are the way they are by God's will, or his divine neglect. Basically it boiled down to *"Thanks, and keep up the good work God! Amen."*

In another section you will find out how effective group prayer is, as proven by Washington, DC having had six days without a murder following a city-wide prayer day. Similarly Orlando, Florida had a reprieve from their body count. Both were specifically attributable to God's intervention as a result of intense coordinated prayers. (Evidently after DC's six days, and Orlando's brief respite from crime, God decided "no more Mr. Nice guy," and the shit hit the fan again. Go figure.)

The same section also offered a heartwarming account of how a father's prayer delivered his son from a shooting on campus, as well as sparing his whole athletic team; proof of the power of prayer. Evidently only non-athletic nerds were killed by the gunman. Thus, one is left to deduce that God responds best to prayers from sports fans, athletes, or athletes' fathers. Nerd's fathers carry no weight with God it seems (no explanation was offered as to why God decided to let sixteen non-athletes be shot to death instead).

If December 7th, 1941, Pearl Harbor Day, is known as the "*date which will live in infamy,*" then the first Thursday in May should be known as the *"day we devote to idiocy;"* when modern day shamans and witch doctors stand before the theistically enslaved and utter their thanks and pleas to the nonexistent figment of their collective ganglia. And the good news is they get to do it again next year.

Next year I'm not going to sit on my hands. No sir! I'm going to do my part by sacrificing a virgin chicken to Tammuz. Hey, when it comes to meaningless gestures of superstitious nonsense, every little bit helps. Besides, I don't want to be branded a Communist.

33

The Ten Commandments: New and Improved

09 May 2008

Well, the Senate resolution (S.Res.483) proposed by the religious fanatic Brownback, to make the first weekend in May "Ten Commandments Weekend," hasn't budged from committee since it was proposed in March. Maybe our Senators aren't total asshats after all. We'll see.

Meanwhile, it occurs to me (as it likely has all of us) that if the Ten Commandments were supposed to be God's directive on how to live our lives, be good and moral people, and ensure the continuity of a civilized world, he sure blew a golden opportunity.

"No other gods," " No graven images," and "Observing the Sabbath" seem to be rather petty and self-serving throwaways given the potential there was to avert a lot of bad human activity into which this god must have surely known we'd lapse.

So I came up with "New and Improved Commandments." Had these been the basis for morality and ethical behavior, perhaps religion would have been superfluous, its renowned excesses avoided, and maybe things wouldn't have gone awry so often. Here they are:

1. **Don't murder folks.**

2. **Slavery is wrong, don't do it.**

3. **Don't take stuff that's not yours.**

4. **Pedophilia is wrong, don't do that.**

5. **Women and Men are equals; afford them equal respect.**

6. **Don't lie, unless by not lying it causes a greater injustice.**

7. **Don't war over imaginary supernatural things, or to spread your version of Utopia to every culture. Save war as the last resort for retaining your freedoms, helping to maintain the freedoms of allies, or preventing genocide.**

8. **Protect the defenseless from those who have no civility.**

9. **Be kind to animals even if you are going to eventually eat them.**

10. **Genetic variances cause racial variation and sexual preference differences. Accept it. Treat everyone as you would be treated.**

No need to live on a mountain for forty days, nor worship any dead minority, or stick your face in the dirt five times a day and mumble your devotion. It's common sense for the ages, it's ethics and morality evolved, simple humanity.

Of course, I have an advantage over the original Ten Commandments authors; I'm not a superstitious-Bronze Age-politically motivated-controlling-genocidal-slavery suborning- homophobic- male chauvinist cultist. I'm just a humble Free Thinking camel.

34

An Expanded Definition of Atheism?

13 May 2008

The dictionary definition of atheist is "a person who denies or disbelieves the existence of a supreme being or beings." I suppose that brief phrase is sufficient, since there is no official dogma or doctrine that atheists hold in common. But based on my experience, some large percent of non-believers do hold in common certain basic principles and philosophies on life.

In 1963, the Supreme Court stopped the practice of prayer in school. Their decision was in response to *Murray v. Curlett*, a suit brought by Madelyn Murray O'Hare, a famous atheist activist widely touted as the most hated woman in America. During that trial the following definition of atheism was given to the Supreme Court by the plaintiff's attorney. It makes a lot of sense:

"Your petitioners are Atheists and they define their beliefs as follows: An Atheist loves his fellow man instead of god. An

Atheist believes that heaven is something for which we should work now – here on earth for all men together to enjoy.

An Atheist believes that he can get no help through prayer but that he must find in himself the inner conviction, and strength to meet life, to grapple with it, to subdue it and enjoy it.

An Atheist believes that only in knowledge of himself and knowledge of his fellow man can he find the understanding that will help to a life of fulfillment. He seeks to know himself and his fellow man rather than to know a god.

An Atheist believes that a hospital should be built instead of a church. An Atheist believes that a deed must be done instead of a prayer said. An Atheist strives for involvement in life and not escape into death. He wants disease conquered, poverty vanquished, war eliminated. He wants man to understand and love man.

He wants an ethical way of life. He believes that we cannot rely on a god or channel action into prayer nor hope for an end of troubles in a hereafter.

He believes that we are our brother's keepers; and are keepers of our own lives; that we are responsible persons and the job is here and the time is now."

It's not perfect, nor would I expect every atheist to subscribe to all of it. I don't necessarily buy into the "brother's keeper" phrase. But it makes a strong distinction between atheism's reality-based ethics, humanity for the sake of humanity, and personal ownership/accountability versus the theist's "pie in the sky" supernatural dependency and abdication of responsibility to a myth.

It evidently had the desired effect on the Supreme Court justices.

35

Those Crazy Christian Zionists

17 May 2008

O n one of George Bush's visits to Israel he alienated the entire Arab world by re-declaring this mystical American-Christian / Israeli-Jewish affinity. Here's an excerpt from the Reuters report:

"Bush, who steps down in January, made little reference to the peace negotiations or to the Palestinians at all while in Israel.

*Many Palestinians were dismayed by a speech to Israel's parliament in which he spoke of a **shared divine providence uniting American Christians like himself with Israel's Jews.***

Bush called Israel a homeland for God's "chosen people" and pledged Washington would remain its "best friend in the world".[1]

"… shared divine providence ??" Let me explain.

I was in Christian chat when "Sean" came into the room and greeted everyone with *"Shalom!"* Strange,

---

[1] http://www.reuters.com/article/worldNews/idUSL1617257200 80516?feedType=RSS&feedName=worldNews

I think, considering this is a "Christian Debate" room, frequented largely by atheists, agnostics and Christians.

I check his profile - he's got an Irish last name and lives in Arkansas. Based on years of experience, I deduce that the likelihood of a Jew having that last name and hailing from Arkansas is somewhere between little and none. So, I ask if he's Jewish. He says *"No, I'm a Christian Zionist."* To be honest, I'd never heard the term before, but I sense immediately where this was leading.

I challenge him. I ask if being a Christian Zionist is just another way of saying he supports Israel because he believes that it will bring about rebuilding of the Temple in Jerusalem, which would lead to the fulfillment of the "End Times" prophesy, the Second Coming, the Rapture, the end of the world? And isn't this "shalom" bullshit, and his professed love for Israel, and his use of the term Zionist, just a thinly veiled disguise for this fundamentalist insanity that seeks the end of the world as we know it according to scripture?

He is shocked and taken aback. He demands to know what right I have, and who gave me the "freedom" to attack him this way? Not to be diverted I ask him to deny that what I say is true. Instead, he becomes agitated, and threatens to leave the room. My invitation for him to do so calms him down and he declares he will not be run off. He offers this: That Israel is the only real democracy and friend of the US in the Middle East, thus he supports Israel.

I offer that I support Israel too, but I don't go around saying *"shalom!"* to total strangers and fellow non-Jews, much less call myself an "Atheist Zionist." I demanded he come clean, again repeating my request for the real intent and meaning of Christian Zionist. He left in a huff.

Here's the bottom line: Christians like these have no more love of Jews or interest in seeing the state of Israel thrive and prosper in peace for the long term than they want to see Satan win the battle of Armageddon. Fundie Christians like that, or like Bush, or Hagee, or Robertson, or Falwell, who declare a strong affinity with the Jewish people and Israel are hypocrites and frauds. To them the State of Israel and the Jews are simply a means to an end, a tool, a catalyst by which their insane End Time prophecies of "Revelation" will be brought about.

What's more, it's so crazy most of them are too embarrassed to admit it.

36

Are We Guaranteed Freedom *From* Religion?

21 May 2008

Often you'll hear Christians say: *"You have the right of Freedom of Religion... not Freedom from Religion"*. Well, as usual they're wrong ... mostly.

The phrase "freedom of religion" is self explanatory. It's the "free exercise clause" of the First Amendment. Practice whatever mindless theology you like as long as its precepts do not violate the laws of the land (i.e. no human sacrifice, no animal cruelty, no polygamy, etc.)

But we also have the freedom not to have a religion and to reject belief in the supernatural. According to Article VI, Section 3 of the US Constitution there can be no "religious test" to hold public office. Thus, since only citizens can hold public office, a lack of belief in God is a guaranteed right to all citizens. The six states whose constitutions still require belief in a supreme being to hold state office have been deemed unconstitutional by the US Supreme Court.

Thus, when George Bush Sr. declared that atheists are *"... not patriots and possibly not even Americans,"* he rejected the Constitutional protection under Article VI, and demonstrated the depth of ignorance that evidently contributed to his son's mental frailties.

Along with the freedom from having to have religion, we also have the freedom/the right to expect that public schools, publicly funded facilities are free of religious teaching, religious symbolism and religious proselytizing. This is where the "Establishment Clause" of the First Amendment comes into play; that "Wall of Separation" phrase that Jefferson coined and that Madison and others echoed.

We have the right to expect that the military services, public symbols, and government agencies are nonsectarian, non-proselytizing, religion neutral, and respectful of the rights of non-believers not to believe.

Finally, we have the right to expect that we be free from the government passing laws that impart favoritism on any religion; free from their spending our tax dollars on religious institutions; free from government promotion of religiosity. It's these points where things tend to get messed with and ignored thanks to religious fanatics in government and their fundie supporters, largely due to their lack of familiarization with, or distortion of, the writings of our Founding Fathers and Supreme Court rulings.

But, theists are correct that our guarantee of freedom from religion is not absolute. Freedom from religion doesn't infer I have the right to expect that I be free from the intrusion of having to see privately funded religious billboards, hear a street preacher, or see crosses on churches; nor should I expect to be freed from having to hear politicians invoke their deity's name, or follow their religious precepts when voting on bills, or appealing to their constituency. That's the right of free speech and the freedom of religion.

In short, a theist's right to Freedom of Religion stops when they try to directly impose their fantasy on me without my expressed consent, or when freedom from government-sponsored religion, in violation of the Constitution, begins.

Everything else relating to the foolishness and ignorance of theist thought and practice is their problem, and their right. There is no law against self delusion or stupidity

37

Curing God's Disease Creations: An Act of Disobedience?

27 May 2008

Ask a Christian why their God created disease and you will get some of the most bizarre responses and tortured reasoning ever devised by human minds. Here are a few common answers actually taken from the internet

> ➤ *"Disease is a curse, so is poverty, addiction and debt. Disobedience by man is what brought on the curse, and separation from God."*

> ➤ *"Germs and viruses didn't harm anyone until Adam and Eve caused death and destruction for us by their disobedience and rebellion."*

> ➤ *"God is pure. God did not create disease, virus or sin, man has."*

> ➤ *"Once Adam and Eve sinned it gave all ownership and rule over the earth to Satan. Satan owns this earth at this point in time. That is why sickness and death and hatred run so high in the world these days."*

> ➤ *"God made disease, and mosquitoes, so that you would know when you were getting sick! These are warning signs for your good."*

What a pathetic jumble of contradictions and convoluted thought. The fact is that if their God created all life on Earth, as they are told in their book of fables, then God's intent is clear: He created germs, viruses and bacteria to plague man as a punishment for sin. Simple.

It wasn't enough to banish Adam and Eve for disobedience, make them earn their bread by the sweat of their brow; make them feel the wrath of the elements, hunger, deprivation, the pain of child birth. No, He's going to inflict his beloved creations with hideous diseases that cause untold pain, suffering, disfiguration and death **for all time.** Seems logical, and oh so loving.

Of course, Christians don't want to piss God off by blaming Him, so Satan, Adam and Eve, or *"it's a good thing,"* is the best way for them to deal with this, thus make the troubling reality of God's hideous diseases go away. It's Christians' way of putting their hands over their ears and shouting *"I can't hear you, I can't hear you!!"*

But there's a bigger question here: If God created these microbes with the intent of making mankind suffer for sin, or if He didn't but allows them to thrive, then surely medical science's fight against disease is an act of rebellion/disrespect toward God and His plan. It's outright heresy to eliminate diseases!!!

Medical science's eradication of small pox and polio is a blatant "in your face" challenge to God, a direct act of disobedience. Research into cures for diseases like AIDS, or Ebola, or flesh eating bacteria, is a slap in the face to the Creator who made them and/or endorses their existence. If God had not intended Man to suffer from diseases, He would not have created or endorsed them. Who is Man to eradicate what God hath created just for him?

Thus, what right does a Christian have to seek inoculations, vaccinations and medical assistance to avoid the devastation of God's microbes? Every flu shot, every polio or small pox inoculation, every antibiotic capsule, every application of Neosporin on a child's cut is an act of disobedience against God's Will. How dare these Christians!?

When faced with this dilemma Christians will often use the escape clause: *"God gave man the ability to discover the cures ... so it's ok."* But that doesn't float because God keeps creating new diseases, new strains, to replace the ones that he allegedly gave science the key to cure or fight. The logic thus doesn't hold up. At best, it infers God likes to develop replacement diseases for the ones He gives science cures for. Plus God seems to really like some of His more grotesque creative exercises, like Muscular Dystrophy, since Jerry Lewis has been raising money to help find a cure for the past 40 years. God obviously wants to hold onto that one.

If Christians continue to allow medical science to ease their ills borne of God's microbial creations, ill's whose pain and death are justifiable retribution for Original Sin, then they are rebelling against their Creator, plain and simple.

They had better stop it now, or there's gonna be Hell to pay.

38
Christians and Criminality Part I: Cons and the Cross

01 Jun 2008

According to various surveys, Christians (all Protestant sects, Catholics, Mormons, JWs, et al) represent between 78% and 83% of the US population. The atheist population is estimated between 8% and 16%.

According to the Federal Bureau of Prisons, Christians represent 83.8% of all convicts in prison, while atheists make up only 0.21% of the prison population.[1]

Thus, Christians make up a disproportionately larger number of convicts to the total Christian population of the US (84% convicts to 80%+ of US population) while atheist convicts make up a disproportionately smaller number to the US atheist population (0.2% convicts to 8%-16% of US population). It's a dramatic difference in the frequency of criminality between believers and non-believers. Considering

---

[1] http://www.holysmoke.org/icr-pri.htm

that Christians claim that without Jesus/God atheists can't have morals or ethics, this is rather shocking.

This leads one to ask the obvious question: If Christians are guided by the word of God; worship a man-god dubbed "the Prince of Peace;" claim to hold a higher moral standard than godless heathens, etc., then how is it they represent such a disproportionately large percentage of the criminal element, while atheists barely register as a blip on the evildoer meter?

Then come the excuses. They'll drag out the ever popular *"But those people aren't REAL Christians."* Naturally that would include Ted Haggard, Warren Jeffs and Jim Bakker; as well as the hundreds of convicted pedophile priests, ministers, and religious youth leaders, et al. Thus, all the Christians in prison aren't *REALLY* Christians, because the *REAL* Christians say they aren't.

The other attempt at denial is *"Well, they converted to Christianity while in prison and weren't Christians when they were convicted."* Naturally there is zero proof or evidence of that. Indeed, while some will "find the Lord"/ become born again in jail, the majority of prison conversions tend to favor Islam as the preferred route, which is the fastest growing religion within the prison system, just as it is in the rest of the world.

Finally, out of desperation, Christians will claim that those who called themselves Christian are really atheists! Evidently, these thousands upon thousands of supposed atheist prisoners have banded together to make Christians look bad ... like that's all they have to worry about in prison.

But the answer is more down to earth and mundane than all that. Christians are typically less educated, come from a lower socio-economic background, are less rational, less intelligent, earn less income, and thus are more likely to be impoverished and turn to crime, than your average atheist. Further, Christians don't have to worry about their personal actions or abiding by man's laws since their dogma guarantees them salvation and forgiveness no matter how many they kill, what they steal, or who they rape. After all, this is just a temporary life on "Satan's Earth," the real reward is to follow, so why not play fast and loose with ethics and morality?

Ever wonder why so many mobsters, biker gangs, Aryan Nation, neo-Nazi groups, gangbangers and Mafioso are Christians? When was the last time you heard of an atheist mob, hate group, or outlaw biker gang or saw a hardcore gangbanger with an atheist symbol tattooed on his forearm? Let me answer for you ... NEVER.

The only question left unanswered is: Are they criminals because of Christianity, or are they Christians because they are criminals? Whichever it is, they sure cause a hell of a lot of misery and pain to society, those god fearing Christian bastions of morality.

39

Christians and Criminality Part II: Ethics and Hypocrisy

04 Jun 2008

I was casually chatting in a Christian debate room when a regular, an especially vapid Evangelical bible banger from Minnesota, tells the room he's going turkey hunting with his son the next morning. On a whim I did a search for Minnesota hunting seasons. Interestingly, turkey season didn't open for another two weeks. I wasn't overly surprised since I knew New Hampshire's season wasn't going to open for a while.

I asked this good Christian how it is that he's going to shoot game out of season. What Would Jesus Say? Isn't it wrong to knowingly break the law, and worse, to teach his son it's okay to ignore conservation laws? His reply was remarkable for its hypocrisy.

"You're not a hunter, you wouldn't understand." [In fact, I hunt small game and have purchased a hunting license every year since I was a teenager except during my military service years. I pushed him again.]

"Why do you bring up Jesus, you're an atheist!!?? Maybe you should let Jesus in your life." [Undeterred by his attempt to obfuscate the issue, I pressed on.]

Finally he blurted this out:

"I've sinned many times in my life; been drunken, used drugs, committed adultery, and hunted out of season & exceeded the limit. Jesus has always forgiven me. He'll forgive me again."

There it was! Even after having admitted premeditated intent to break the law; even while knowing he's setting a bad example for his son; even realizing that he has admitted to a chat room full of people that he has no regard for conservation law, or respect for the preservation of game species, he justified it because *Jesus has always forgiven him and will again … tomorrow.*

This is what passes for Christian morality and ethics. Indeed, it's a contributing factor to why Christians are more prone to criminal activity and represent a disproportionately higher population of prison inmates than atheists: They get a pass, a clean slate from their God over and over again, they just have to ask.

Yet I, an atheist, who acts in accordance with the law, shows respect for game by harvesting them only in season, who would no more teach my son to do otherwise than I would teach him how to steal a car, I am the "heathen" bereft of ethics and morals?

If only I had my own imaginary man-god to cleanse me of my crimes. Then I too could act like a mindless slob hunter and unethical law-breaking scumbag with impunity. I guess being theist has its benefits.

40

Can Religious Fable and Science be Reconciled? Should it be?

08 Jun 2008

An ex-Catholic, now-agnostic acquaintance made the following statement:

"There is no need for fighting between religion and science. There is plenty of room within the various stories and fables of the religions for science to fit in."

I couldn't disagree more.

Trying to reconcile miraculous myths by proffering natural phenomenon or scientific explanations is an exercise in the absurd. Things like the Nile turning red (*"Oh...it was an earthquake that released clay into the river."*); or the frog plague (*"Oh... a water spout could have caused that."*); or Moses staff turning into a snake and eating the other staff/snakes of the Egyptian priests (*"Oh...well... uh... that could have been an optical illusion caused by....yada, yada, yada."*). Please. One might as well justify how Superman "could possibly" fly given the right wind currents and a properly tailored cape.

When one tries to find a scientific explanation for a mythical non-natural event, things get stickier:

1) What is the scientific basis for, or where does science fit into, the Resurrection of Jesus, or his raising of Lazarus?

2) What physical law observed by science permits the fabled feeding of the multitude by miraculously multiplying a finite number of fish and loaves?

3) What is the scientific explanation for water being instantly converted into fermented grape juice?

4) How does our scientific knowledge about geology and the universe support the mythical places known as Hell and Heaven?

Answers: 1-3 there is none; 4 it doesn't. But if you're going to toss out "woulda, coulda, shoulda" natural causes for *some* unnatural fables, where do you draw the line? How is proffering a natural explanation for the Nile turning red reasonable, but outright rejection of the rising of a decomposed corpse isn't?

Why is this important? Because these myths are the basis for faith of the theistically impaired. It is their justification for Jesus' divinity, and establishes the mythical realms of eternal reward and punishment in exchange for acceptance or denial of their preferred myth. It is those myths that have given rise to almost 2000 years of mind enslavement, horror and injustice, and their continued acceptance promulgates it.

Thus, there is no room in genuine science, or compelling justification, to cut and fit natural law/scientific theory so it is accommodated within religious fantasy in order to give that fantasy a semblance of plausibility. Real science trumps religious fantasy, dispels it, supplants it, and renders it unsupportable fiction.

Science's tenets and principles have increased man's knowledge, brought him out of the darkness of ignorance and superstition, have reduced the size of the "God of the Gaps" and eventually should bring about its virtual demise. And when it does, religious exclusionism, intolerance, homophobia, misogyny, ignorance and attempts at theocratic supremacy will go with it.

Trying to make scientific sense of supernatural tales plays into the hands of theists. In the struggle of science vs. myth, reason vs. ignorant blind belief, there can be no accommodation, no middle ground. Pick your side.

41

Does a Candidate's Belief Affect His Fitness to Govern?

12 Jun 2008

Recently, a blogger whom I respect and whose opinion I value, said that even if Obama were Muslim it wouldn't stop him from voting for him. While I respect his position, I don't share that philosophy. I could not vote for a Muslim for President any more than I could vote for a Christian fundamentalist (again!), a devotee of Voodoo, a Satanist, a Scientologist, or any other belief system outside the culturally mainstream moderate-liberal, middle-of-the-road Judeo-Christian, or atheist candidate.

Putting aside the admittedly emotional elements surrounding Muslims, it reminds me of the statement often fronted by Christian fundies in defense of their most theistically infected Republican Party standard bearers: *"A person's religious belief has no effect on their competence of holding that office."*

Sorry, I don't buy it. In fact truth be told, they don't buy it either. Their position presupposes that the candidate is Christian. Their magnanimous position would evaporate in a heartbeat if the person was Hindu or a Heavens Gate cultist. It's just more hypocrisy from the Christian Right. The difference between my rejection of certain candidates for holding certain beliefs, or the intensity of their belief, is upfront and on the table. No hypocrisy there.

Some might say: *"But, your decrying theist rejection of atheist candidates is hypocrisy, since you yourself reject certain people based on belief. You're being inconsistent. "* But they'd be mistaken. Since atheism isn't a belief/belief system, their statement that *"...religious belief has no effect on competency to hold office"* is antithetical to an atheist candidate (not that there are any admitted atheist candidates). Certainly any political, social, or ethical positions an atheist holds should be – and are – open to scrutiny as to suitability to govern, but not his atheism, per se, since it is not a belief. It's simply a *lack of belief.*

An atheist candidate would have no supernaturally driven agenda. There could be no split allegiance between upholding the laws of man (Common Law/the Constitution), and some "Higher Moral Authority" handed down by some fictional divine being or prophet. There is only The Law, evolved human ethics, and culturally acceptable morality. Unlike theists, there is no conflict in the atheist mind, and no chance of decision making being based on prophesy or bizarre doctrine that welcomes or hastens Armageddon, or that may offend the sensibilities of a mythical supreme being, or that is interpreted as having been God-sent or divinely endorsed.

Thus, where no Constitutional amendment exists that permits government to interfere with beneficial scientific advancement (i.e. stem cell research, animal cloning); or medical advancements (i.e. the distribution of the Human Papilloma Virus preventative vaccine, or over-the-counter sale of morning after contraceptives); then an atheist has neither lawful nor logical reason to impede those things which may contribute to the common good and improve the human condition.

Where the Constitution has never been interpreted to impede the right of the terminally ill to die a dignified death and end ones interminable suffering, or to prevent people of the same sex from marrying, then the governing atheist's position would be unencumbered by some nonsensical question like *"What Would Jesus Do?"* or *"What did the bronze age writers of the Old Testament have to say on the matter?"* or *"Lets consult the Koran."*

While theists might perceive atheists as a threat to the free practice of their religion, such an opinion has no evidentiary support. It would be in direct contradiction to the Constitutional guarantees of the First Amendment to which any American atheist would subscribe.

I hold that any supernatural/mythical belief held by a candidate potentially puts that candidate in conflict with governing in accordance with the law, reason and good sense. My position is simple: All other qualifications being equal, in lieu of an atheist, the less religious, and the more main stream/liberal the religious flavor of the candidate, the better off we all are. Eight years of George W. Bush supports that contention.

42

Gun Rights Bestowed by GOD!

15 Jun 2008

I have a confession to make: I'm a member of the National Rifle Association (NRA). I have been since I was thirteen years old. As an avid gun collector and informal target shooter, it behooves me to contribute to an organization whose primary objective is to ensure I continue to have the right to pursue my hobby.

But, unfortunately, my membership puts me in the company of some really weird folks. I'd venture that a vast majority of fundies are members of the NRA. That doesn't diminish the value of the organization, it just embarrasses me.

Today I received the NRA's monthly magazine *The American Rifleman* , a benefit of membership. I flipped through the technical articles, the collector's section, the section on examples of Americans who legally defended their lives and property with guns, etc. Then I came to the "Letter from the President" column. Here the president of the NRA gives his monthly inspirational talk.

This month he wrote on the Presidential election. As one would expect, he came down hard on Obama and Clinton, and their strong anti-gun stance. I know all this, and have decided to vote for Obama anyway. My reasoning being that given the direction this country has gone, and is going, under a Republican/theistically beholding administration, it's time for me to put my personal interests aside for the good of the Nation as a whole. I don't know if Obama and the Democrats will be the answer to the country's woes, but it's unlikely it can be worse than another Republican administration. In the event any misguided knee-jerk gun legislation is proposed under an Obama administration, I will do what I have always done: Actively letter write, stay politically involved, and trust that the NRA and Congress will prevent well-intentioned but utterly stupid gun laws from passing that will do nothing to reduce crime but would impinge on my Constitutionally guaranteed gun ownership rights.

But here's the clincher. In the NRA president's column comes this statement: ***"Gun ownership is a God-given Right."*** I'm stunned. Picture a camel with his jaw hanging open.

Forget about the fact that the Founding Fathers didn't include mention of God when they wrote the Constitution, not even once and many of them were Deists who totally rejected the concept of a Creator intervening in Man's affairs.

Don't consider the fact that if the gun rights granted under the Second Amendment are divinely provided, then one has to logically assume that the Twenty-first Amendment, which repealed the prohibition of alcohol, was also the work of God, as are presumably all other Constitutional amendments.

Never mind that by inferring gun ownership is endorsed by a deity that NOT owning a gun would, logically, be a blasphemous insult to this gun-loving God.

Ignore the little detail that the Bible never once mentions the right to own arms, much less guns.

Yes, forget and discount all that and just realize that the very statement of *"God-given right"* infers supernatural justification for and endorsement of, gun ownership, and thus puts the Second Amendment on a par with the Ten Commandments, kosher dietary law and the admonishment in the Old Testament to stone your unruly children!

One can only wonder if this "God-given right" extends to felons and terrorists, much less Muslims, pagans, and atheists. After all, *they is all God's chil'en.* Maybe it's just applicable to law-abiding Christian US citizens, maybe even Jews. But who's to know since God evidently hasn't seen fit to inform us of his perspective on who qualifies to pack iron. No doubt the president of the NRA, evidently God's chosen prophet on matters pertaining to firearms, could advise us of God's position on that. Then the only question left is WGWJO?[1]

The stupidity I have to endure as a member of this organization is disturbing.

---

[1] What Guns Would Jesus Own

43

What's More Christian than a Good Old Fashioned Book Burning?

19 Jun 2008

Well, to be honest, Jewish persecution, as well as the murder and subjugation of indigenous peoples is MORE Christian, but let's not split hairs; book burning is right up there when listing Christian proclivities toward institutionalized barbaric behavior.

Wiki lists fifty-nine of the most infamous book burning episodes in history. It goes back as early as the 3rd century BCE and as recently as May 2008.[2] It lists acts of book burning in Asia, the Middle East, Europe, America, the Far East, virtually the entire world, or more succinctly, what we refer to as "the Civilized World," by various cultures. While certainly not a complete list of every such event, it captures the most historically noteworthy.

---

[2] http://en.wikipedia.org/wiki/Book_burning#Christian_books_
.28by_Diocletian.29

Interestingly, but not surprisingly, twenty-three of these acts of book burning, almost 40%, were by Christians, both Catholics and Protestants. The subject matter of the volumes that drew their ire was diverse: Science, philosophy, competing interpretations of Christian doctrine (aka heretical texts), Jewish texts, fiction, history, and various "black arts." Among the most recent examples was an organized *Harry Potter* book incineration and family values cookout.

Today, Christian book burnings are more show and symbolic acts of ignorance and intolerance. With the internet and other forms of transmitting thought and opinion, book burning is an inefficient method of silencing free thought. The early book burnings, however, were more than symbolic. They were intended to obliterate any competing information or position, whether factual or opinion, that was counter to the teachings of the Church. It was meant to completely eradicate such thought so as to prevent it from becoming known and spread. For if knowledge became accessible to the masses; if dissenting thought became rooted; if people began to question doctrine and thought mandated by the Church hierarchy, then the power base of the Church becomes undermined, and its source of sustenance jeopardized.

Many volumes were lost to history. In a few notable cases, like Michael Servetus, 16th century physician and discoverer of the human circulatory system, the author was burned alive by the Church along with what was believed to be the last volume of his heretical work chained to his leg. Fortunately, three volumes of his dissertation against the non-Biblical doctrine of the Trinity, and for a purer and kinder flavor of Christianity survived. It only cost him his life.

Servetus' thoughts live on in his book, and through Unitarianism.

While totalitarian governments and other religions are guilty of similar acts of intolerance and barbarism in their thirst to retain power and suppress free thought, not one institution, not one other religion, not one single nation or political persuasion throughout history comes close to Christianity in pure volume of book burnings over such a sustained period of time. It continues to this day.

If prizes were awarded for suppressing ideas, attempting to control people's thoughts, keeping people in ignorance, and destroying civilization's most revered source of knowledge, Christianity would win hands down. Congratulations Christianity, we knew you had it in you.

44

Is Atheist Dismissal of Theists Wrong?

23 Jun 2008

I had a nice exchange with a "halfway realist" Christian recently. I say "halfway", because he has accommodated science with his superstition, as so many liberal Christians have been doing. He accepts Evolutionary theory, and I sense he questions the efficacy of modern day belief in miracles, and the mystical aspects of theism, but just can't quite make the final step into reality yet.

In the course of our exchange he decried the tendency of atheists to get angry at Christians, and to dismiss Christians and their beliefs out of hand. What follows is my response to him.

I only get angry when fundies try to dumb down our schools with Creationism under the guise of the pseudo-science called Intelligent Design; or when Christian moral dictates from their supreme being impinge on the freedoms of others; or when they distort genuine science in an attempt to justify myth; or when government picks my pocket to suborn religious organizations. Otherwise, I just make fun of them as a hobby.

As for my dismissal of Christians, theists in general, and the supernaturalism that goes with it, they are not alone. I am dismissive of people who invest their lives in conspiracy theories that are unsubstantiated; people who believe the government is concealing extra terrestrial alien activity on Earth; or those who think the US government contrived 9/11 for some nefarious purpose. I am dismissive of people who to this day believe we never landed on the moon; believe that the pyramids were built by aliens and believe that witches are real, that sorcery exists, or that Bigfoot roams the woods.

I imagine that you dismiss many, if not most of these things as well, in spite of the degree of genuine belief, delusion, or enthusiasm that drives these people. As a believer you may reject these examples as being entirely dissimilar to YOUR religious belief and thus think your perspective is less deserved of dismissal. But, as one who views all fable, all myth, all flights of fancy and inventions of the mind the same way, there is not one iota of difference to me.

Do people have the right to these absurd thoughts and beliefs? Absolutely.

Do their beliefs deserve my respect? No. They warrant only my dismissal at best, ridicule at worst.

Your religious belief is no less deserved of my dismissal than any other unsupportable, un-provable, un-testable, un-substantiated belief/belief system grounded in fantasy and bereft of evidence. I owe it no more respect, and it deserves no less dismissal, than the practice of Aztec sacrifice to the Sun God, or belief that the goddess Athena sprang from the head of Zeus.

That you and many other Christians have been able to accept scientific proofs and incorporate them into your belief system, creating a hybrid, as it were, between total dependency on supernatural, and total acceptance of reality is a good thing. I welcome and commend it. I see it as a step in the demise of religion that began some 300 years ago with the advent of the scientific age, and that will eventually end with supernaturalism's disappearance.

That you can't just acknowledge the teachings attributed to Jesus the man as a refinement of morality and good guide for civilization, but must retain that illogical grasp on blind belief in mysticism, is tantamount to why we still have a vestigial tail, and body hair. Eventually, those too will pass.

45

Religion and Business: Playing Fundies to Your Advantage

26 Jun 2008

Some weeks ago I placed an order for a specialty item from a firm in the Midwest. While searching their website I found one of those insipid "Jesus is Our Lord and Savior" testimonials on one of their pages. It screamed "Fundie!!"

Now normally, I wouldn't deal with religious nuts that don't have the intellect, or good sense, to separate their business reality from their religious fantasy, but they are the only source for their patented product. I shrugged, dialed the phone and placed my order.

Anna was knowledgeable and friendly. She warned me each unit was made to order and could take up to four weeks, since it's a small family business. They will, however, be charging my credit card immediately. Okay.

Five weeks later, nothing. I called and ask for Anna. She apologized and said it would be another week. Fine. Ten days pass, still no delivery. I called again but this time with a plan. Here's the conversation, verbatim:

Me*: "Hi Anna, this is Hump from New Hampshire."*

Anna: *"Oh, yes, hello."*

Me: *"I was wondering how my order was coming."*

Anna*: "Oh, yes … let me check on that."*

[on hold for a full minute]

Anna: *"Sorry Hump, Tim hasn't gotten to it, but it should be within a week or two."*

Me [pissed off but hiding it under my sanctimonious love of Jesus]: *"That's ok, Anna, Jesus has blessed me with patience. God Bless you and Tim. If there's anything you can do to help speed …"*

Anna [interrupting me]: *"Hump, can you hold on for one second please?*

[on hold for 20 seconds]

Anna: *"Tim says he will have this done and in the mail to you this afternoon."*

Me: *"God Bless you, Anna. Thanks so much!"*

Anna: *"And may the Good Lord bless and keep you as well, Hump. Bye."*

Now, I suppose it could have been just my good luck that Tim miraculously found the time to complete my order that day, after having put me off just seconds before. But I think not. It's obvious my "devotion" to Jesus moved them.

I suppose a theist would say I was being deceptive by intentionally misrepresenting myself as a Christian in order to gain favor. My perspective, however, is entirely different. Much like the ancient pagan priests used their knowledge of celestial movements to predict natural events to impress and subdue their weak-minded people, I simply used my knowledge of fanatical Christians' own weaknesses to my benefit. Why should a business give preference to a customer because they think they share a superstition in common? And if they do, aren't they themselves being "un-Christian" in their business practice?

Besides, they are already operating under a delusion. One more induced by a far away disembodied camel won't harm them one bit.

46

Scientists, a Teapot, and Consideration of a Possible God

06 Jul 2008

My Christian pen pal suggested that great scientists can be theists, and that famous contemporary activist atheists are too "fundamentalist" to leave any room for the possibility of God. My reply:

Yes, Christians like F.S. Collins, a respected scientist and head of the genome project, are rarities. That Collins is able to compartmentalize his belief so that it is kept distinct and separate from his scientific impartiality is an accommodation that is unusual and commendable. But, it's not by coincidence that upwards of 93-96% of the most respected scientists in the world in the "hard disciplines," the members of the UK's Royal Society of Science, and its American counterpart, the National Academy of Science, claim no belief in God(s). Collins falls into the remaining 4 - 7%. It makes him an anomaly among his peers.

As for room for belief in God(s) among atheists you are wrong in saying Dawkins and Hitchens et al have zero ability to accept the possibility of God, along with all the traditional supernatural accoutrements (i.e. heaven, hell, angels, demons, Satan, etc.). I am, and I'm very sure that they are, willing to reserve the exact same amount of credulity for such things as you are in accepting the existence of "Russell's Teapot."

Refreshing your memory, allow me to paraphrase (and embellish) Bertrand Russell's Celestial Teapot concept. It proposes that a tiny teapot, fine porcelain I believe, is in elliptical orbit around the sun between Earth and Mars. It's white, with a Wedgewood blue lid. This teapot can't be seen, or detected in anyway. That there is no verifiable evidence of its existence, that the mechanism for its existence is unknown, does not dismiss its possible existence. The fact that we can imagine its existence, record its qualities, and declare its possibility is good enough to attribute some degree of likelihood of existence, however small or remote.

The percentage of likelihood that you are willing to attribute to Russell's Teapot actually existing is very close to the percentage of likelihood that Dawkins, Hitchens, I and most "strong atheists" are willing to attribute to the possibility of the existence of a supernatural being and Its/His/Her complimentary supernatural accoutrements. However, I'm quite sure that you'd require some very extraordinary, hard, objective, and compelling evidence to convince you to believe that tea pot actually exists. So would I. That's because extraordinary claims require extraordinary evidence.

Yet strangely, while I (and Hitchens, Dawkins, Harris, et al.) need the exact same level of hard and compelling objective evidence to convince us of an undetectable God as we would need to accept Russell's teapot, YOU accept God/supernaturalism with no more hard and objective evidence than you have for that teapot. That is inconsistency, a breakdown in reasoning that strong atheists, millions of free thinkers, including myself, do not suffer from. That inconsistency, prevalent among theists, is illogical, albeit we know that "faith" in God without evidence, like faith in cosmic teapots without evidence, defies logic.

Those alien advocates, conspiracy theorists, Young Earthers, Flat Earthers, ESP advocates, etc., who need no hard evidence to justify their beliefs, pretty much are placed in the same realm as Christians and theists in general, as far I am concerned. I'd proffer that 93-96% of the best scientific minds on the planet would agree. Atheists have room to believe in a god, we just need the objective evidence.

47

Life, Salvation, and Suicide

09 Jul 2008

"If you don't believe in God and salvation, what do you have to live for? Why don't you just kill yourself now?"

This is a favored fundie Christian retort when they find themselves angered by their unsuccessful attempts to recruit heathens, or when frustrated in debate when defense of their childlike fable is ineffective against the onslaught of logic and science. One can almost see their faces contorted in anger, their spittle forming foamy masses in the corners of their mouths.

I find the very premise of the statement irrational. Where rests the logic behind why anyone who savors this short life as the only life one has want to kill himself?

What do I have to live for? For life itself! My life finds fulfillment in the love of my wife and family, the camaraderie of my friends, my dogs, my favorite hobbies, reading, eating good food in copious amounts, parties, celebrating births, sharing the sorrows and easing the burdens of my loved ones, participating in community service, warm days in the sun, cool evenings around the fire, trips to Home Depot, an occasional Whopper from Burger King, life's daily trials, tribulations and challenges, etc. All of it is what contributes to making life enjoyable, meaningful and worth living for as long as is comfortable and reasonably possible. How can the obvious logic of this elude fundamentalist Christians?

No. The appropriate logic is quite the reverse of fundie Christian illogic. Since Christians see this life as only a brief training ground for their eternity in Candy Land, imagining themselves as smiling zombies groveling on their knees, performing Dog knows what acts of servitude and humiliation for their imaginary Slave Master Super Being, aren't *THEY* the ones who would benefit by hurrying the termination of their evidently burdensome and less than satisfactory lives? Why would they stick around in this imperfect material world when there is something better than this life awaiting them in the next?

I, for one, encourage them to seek their reward, sooner rather than later.

48

Rogues Gallery: Top Ten List of the Worst Christian Clergy

12 Jul 2008

It's almost as though being a mindless, blithering buffoon is a prerequisite to become a public figure clergyman in this country.

The latest example was an utterance by the Reverend Jesse "Mumbles" Jackson, defaming Obama, and causing Jesse's own Congressman son to dismiss him as a veritable jerk. It wasn't Jesse's first gaff. Years ago he showed his true colors by referring to New York City as "Hymie Town," among other anti-Semitic slurs. The fact that this sanctimonious paragon of Christian morality fathered children via a mistress, and that in 2001 he had some questionable financial transactions involving his Rainbow Coalition salary become public, all pretty much point to an inarticulate loose cannon with little class, few scruples and even less intellect. But this kind of behavior isn't unique to Jesse. It's epidemic among men of the cloth in the public eye.

Let's put aside the obvious charlatans, whose tent revivals and fake healings are geared to mentally impaired sucker believers. They don't qualify as clergy. As far as I am concerned, these are entrepreneurs who see a business opportunity and maximize its potential by separating the most gullible Christians from their welfare checks. They prove the old maxim that "a fool and his money are soon parted." It's free market capitalism.

And I won't dredge up the hundreds and hundreds of priests, pastors, youth ministers, deacons and assorted church officials, who, cloaked in godliness, use their position of authority and trust to rape and molest children. That's a whole different level of sub-human clergy, albeit their numbers seem to be growing.

No, I'm talking about the theist "leaders," the public political shamans, the master shearers of the sheep who have risen to the top of the steaming pile of theist misanthropes. Those who declare God's political preferences, speak for Him and who rely on guile, bad theology and a bombastic presence to transfix their followers, while sacrificing intellect, integrity, humility, honesty, dignity and their humanity. These are the darlings of the media and the masses of bleating theist sheep. A media circus unto themselves, they are the antithesis of the Jesus they claim to worship and represent.

Here, along with Jesse, is my Top Ten List of Clergy Low Life in no particular order:

"Reverend" Jeremiah Wright: Obama's ex-pastor who has expressed racist comments, irrational conspiracy theories, and anti- American slogans. A self promoting raging fanatic and beloved minister of the hallelujah crowd.

"Reverend" Jerry Falwell: Rabid homophobe; promoter of the concept that AIDS is God's punishment on society for tolerating homosexuality; the guy who blamed 9/11 on America's Sodom and Gomorrah ways. Happily he's dead now, albeit, not soon enough for my liking.

"Reverend" Al Sharpton: He of the "Jewish interloper" comment; the Tawana Brawley fake racial incident; the trumped up accusations of racism against anyone who opposes his demagoguery and instigations of countless inflammatory and unnecessary confrontations. A rabble-rousing, race-baiting publicity hound, whose IQ is rivaled by his waist size and the number of ounces of grease he slathers into his hair.

"Reverend" Pat Robertson: Where to start? ... How about this quote?: *"The feminist agenda is not about equal rights for women. It is about a socialist, anti-family political movement that encourages women to leave their husbands, kill their children, practice witchcraft, destroy capitalis, and become lesbians."* There is an unending supply of similarly inane comments, many even worse. A true man of peace, Pat has called openly for the assassination of foreign leaders. A homophobe par excellence, he blamed hurricane Katrina's devastation of New Orleans on the city's evil ways, saying it was the wrath of God. He'll also sell you his God-given recipe for an energy drink that will give you the "strength of Samson." Perhaps the most unstable of the lot, Robertson is dangerous and a living, breathing example of Elmer Gantry run amok.

"Reverend" Jimmy Swaggart: Pentecostal TV hypocrite who was influential in exposing TV competitor Jim Bakker's sexual indiscretions. Two years later he himself was caught with a hooker, twice. His ministry is marked by thoughtful comments like this: *"Sex education classes in our public schools are promoting incest."*

"Reverend" Jim Bakker: Another defrocked TV minister, caught in a sex scandal, and convicted of accounting fraud with his own Evangelical church funds, the "love offerings" of his zombie flock. Having done hard time in prison, he is still broadcasting TV shows to his God-fearing and unshakable followers while he tries to pay down the $6 million he owes the IRS.

"Reverend" Ted Haggard: Raging homophobe and disgraced Evangelical leader, he was caught buying crystal meth and boffing a male prostitute. After entering "homosexual rehab" for two weeks he claimed to have been "cured of [his] illness," The Evangelical leadership didn't buy it. Many of his least intelligent Christian sheep do.

"Reverend" Billy Graham: This fire and brimstone tent preacher rose to prominence as Minister to Presidents. Presenting himself as the paragon of tolerance and inclusion, he was accused of anti-Semitic statements made in conversation with President Nixon. He vehemently denied it as a total fabrication. Unfortunately for him it was all on Oval Office audio tape, which was released to the media. Busted as a Jew hater and liar, he prefers to continue to deny any memory of the conversation. The internet death pool has him at even odds of joining Falwell by 2010.

"Reverend" John Hagee: Endorsed McCain for President. McCain happily accepted this Evangelical bigwig's support, until he found out Hagee refers to the Catholic Church as "The Great Whore," and to the Holocaust as a "good thing" for the Jewish people in the long run. Ooops!!!

Now, I'm not suggesting all clergy are like this. Many, perhaps most of them, are fine people who do some good, in spite of their religious infirmity. But the facts are plain: The higher a Man of the Cloth rises in the public arena, the more likely he is to be exposed for the fraud and hateful hypocrite he is. If being an intellectually deficient hypocrite is not a prerequisite, it's certainly an acquired trait among the most visible of God's self-appointed agents. It lends credence to the old saying: *"Scratch a preacher and you'll find a sinner."* … and a hypocrite.

49

Does Religiosity Influence Quality of Life?

15 Jul 2008

The latest Pew Poll reports that New Hampshire, my state, is tied with Vermont for the least religious state in the Union. Only 54% of New Hampshire residents have certainty that God exists. Compare that to the most religious state, Mississippi, where 91% are certain there is a God.

On the question of the importance of religion in ones life, only 36% of New Hampshire residents feel it's important. On the other end of the spectrum, 82% of Mississippians rate religion important. Here's an extract of the whole report. You can also check your state's religiosity level: http://vyoma108.blogspot.com/2008/06/religion-in-america-massachusetts-among.html

These statistics reflect a very significant difference in the number of believers between NH and MS. Certainly, with theist claims of a higher morality, Mississippians might suspect that New Hampshire is a den of iniquity, a veritable Sodom and Gomorrah compared to the God fearing Jesus freaked state of Mississippi.

But, not surprisingly, the complete opposite is true. Let's examine the facts:

While New Hampshire had the 4th lowest violent crime rate in the country, Mississippi was the 21st highest in violent crime. http://www.morganquitno.com/dango6.htm

NH is ranked as the state with the least number of people below the poverty level. Mississippi has the second highest number of people in poverty in the country. http://www.census.gov/statab/ranks/rank34.html

The average calculated IQ of the populace of the state of NH is 104.2, the second highest IQ of all states (Massachusetts was first with 104.3). Compare this to Mississippi's IQ of 94.2, the lowest IQ average of any State in the Union! http://www.people.vcu.edu/~mamcdani/Publications/McDaniel%20(2006)%20Estimating%20state%20IQ.pdf

Divorce rate for NH is 3.3 per 1,000 people, below the national average of 3.6. For Mississippi it's 4.5 per 1,000 people, or 36% higher than NH and higher than the national average. http://www.infoplease.com/ipa/A0923080.html

Finally, teen pregnancy in NH is second lowest in the country. Mississippi has the nation's third highest rate. http://www.guttmacher.org/pubs/2006/09/12/USTPstats.pdf

So what does this all mean? Well, the differences are certainly intriguing, and should cause the religiously afflicted to rethink their sanctimonious misconceptions about the impact religion has on the quality of life, morality, family values, et al.

To be fair, there exists any number of factors other than, or in addition to, religiosity that could influence these results. Thus, as thinking people, and adherents to the scientific method, we cannot simply accept that high religiosity influences higher crime, higher poverty, lower intelligence levels, more teen pregnancies, etc. Not with certainty, not based on this simple analysis. In fact its possible that a state's lower standard of living, quality of life, intelligence level, et al, are a cause of increased religiosity.

But I'll tell you this: Given the circumstantial evidence, the fact that these results hold true for comparisons between virtually every other non-religious versus religious state, I'd avoid living in the Bible Belt like the plague. Mississippi wouldn't be among my top 49 choices. I'd pick a state where the least number of people believe in angels and devils, talk in tongues, handle snakes, symbolically consume their Man-god, walk around praising the Lord, or waving their hands and falling down in spasms of hyper-religious ecstasy every Sunday. In other words, the less religious the state the better, assuming quality of life is an important factor to you.

I am going to suggest New Hampshire change its state motto from *"Live Free or Die"* to *"Land of the Godless, and Loving it."*

50

The Charming Atheist: A Little Good PR Can't Hurt

18 Jul 2008

Ask a church-going Christian what their perception of an atheist is and you'd likely get a list of attributes that would just as well describe Joe Stalin, Pol Pot, or Jason the hockey-masked fiend from the *Friday the 13*th movies. So I feel it my duty when interacting face-to-face with theists, and when compelled to divulge my non-belief, to put my best hump forward.

I recently had my annual visit from the Jehovah's Witnesses. I was on the patio working on my tan, reading Hitchens' *god is not Great*, when they rolled down my driveway. I greeted them, and went into my usual routine, which includes introducing them to the dogs, and offering them a cold drink and use of the bathroom facilities.

I let them do their spiel for a few minutes then, after turning down their pamphlet, declared my atheism, showed them my current reading material and told them they are always welcome to stop by for the restroom or a soft drink. They were naturally shocked, probably as much by my friendliness and hospitality as by the fact that I didn't have horns and didn't try to kill and eat them. They smiled nervous smiles, thanked me, piled into the car and left. I waved as they rolled down the driveway. Each year it's a new group. It's always fun.

Today I went to the supermarket with a short list. Outside the entrance there was a card table staffed by two women selling raffle tickets for their church. I asked what the money would go toward, and was told that their church is trying to raise money to buy fuel oil for less fortunate families. With the price of oil twice what it was last year, and the harsh New Hampshire winters, it's a very good and necessary cause. The top three raffle prizes are gasoline cards for $100, $75 and $50. I bought six tickets for $5.00.

I filled out the stubs, and on the back of each I wrote that should my tickets be drawn, the winnings should go back into the fuel oil fund, and I signed my name. When they saw this they were overwhelmed and thanked me profusely. That's when they asked to what church I belonged. Uh-oh!

Now that kind of comment, obviously borne of the belief that only a fellow believer could possibly make a charitable gesture, might have irked me. I fought back the instinct to chastise them for their erroneous assumption. Instead, I smiled and offered: *"No church, ladies … I'm an atheist. I trust my contribution is still acceptable?"* Without even a hint of disgust, nor the telltale crossing of themselves, nor even an attempt to throw holy water on me, they smiled back and assured me it was very much accepted and greatly appreciated.

The moral of this is, given the opportunity to show that atheists are as moral, ethical, charitable, hospitable and decent as any of them – likely even more so – take it. Eventually there will be more of us than there are of them. Until then, a little good PR couldn't hurt.

51

Christianity the Cult of Death

22 Jul 2008

Ever notice how so much of the doctrine and focus of Christianity revolves around their obsession with death and dying? It is the driving force behind their entire belief system. It pervades their thinking and is endemic to their dogma. Let's examine the facts:

Christians fully endorse the acts of genocide, infanticide, enslavement and mass killing of humans and animals depicted in the Old Testament as God-directed or inspired. It is deemed justified and good because it was God's will.

From there it centers on their man-god's death by crucifixion and zombie-like reanimation; Jesus as willing human-deity sacrifice, the "Lamb of God;" Jesus as a substitute for the burnt animal offering of the early Hebrews and pagan rites. Jesus worship centers more on his violent, bloody, tortured and alleged willing death than his life or alleged teachings.

Indeed, they flock to the theaters to watch Mel Gibson's slasher film *The Passion of The Christ* to vicariously drench themselves in the gallons of fake blood and flayed skin, offered as a grotesque, over-the-top reenactment of what thousands of Jews went through during Rome's occupation of Israel. Just as Easter passion plays do, the blood bath makes them feel refreshed and renewed; it has a cathartic effect, like vampires satiated after feeding.

They practice symbolic cannibalism, drinking their man-god's blood, eating his body. Again, the vampire theme.

The cross, an instrument of violent death, is their symbol. Catholics like it best with a bloody corpse hanging from it. I'd guess that if there was a Jesus and he saw his teachings represented by a death device he'd be disgusted and repelled.

Catholics also revere an imitation death shroud, and the severed body parts, "relics," of dead martyrs.

Some Christian sects withhold medical technology and pharmaceuticals from their children and placidly accept their death because it's "God's will." Others handle poisonous snakes in a bizarre dance of death, re-enacting a scriptural passage which promises true believers they won't die from the bite. Many do.

Christians refer to the imaginary place where their dead go as "a better place." Thus better to be dead than alive.

Will they beam up in the Rapture, when graves will open and the dead will rise? Will they be left behind to suffer a hideous existence on Earth? Will they be good enough to live for ever in Candy Land with Jesus? Will they be sent to Hell, tormented and tortured for an eternity by a hideous demon without ever the hope of relief? How much time after death will they spend in Purgatory? It's all tied up in one enormous obsession with death and dying.

Not being satisfied with their own obsession, they threaten non-believers with their imaginary Hell after death, as though our minds are of the same Play-Doh consistency as theirs. In Revelations it says the saved in Heaven will get to watch the hideous torments of those in Hell, like a bizarre sadistic spectator sport, a reward for the faithful. Charming.

Over the centuries they have, in the name of Jesus, put to death Jews, Muslims, fellow Christians declared as heretics, "witches," non-believers, indigenous pagan peoples, gynecologists and homosexuals in hideous ways, in the name of Jesus, and in monumental numbers, for their God willed it or scripture prescribes or condones it.

Christians endorse war in greater numbers than do non-believers or any other belief system save perhaps Muslims, as though it's some sort of sacrament. Sometimes they invoke the name of the Crusades as their call to war, the Crusades being the quintessential example of Christian mass murder and a travesty to civilization. With the words "God is on our side" they justify war as divinely endorsed.

While they despise Jews in private for their rejection of their man-god, and Christianity is the basis for anti-Semitic thinking and with it Jewish persecution and misery for almost 2000 years, in public they support the Jews of Israel. They pray for Israel to vanquish the Arabs in the hopes of rebuilding The Temple in Jerusalem. In so doing they believe it will fulfill their death wish End Times prophesy, bring about Armageddon and the end of life on Earth as we know it, which they welcome with open arms.

Death, pain, holy war, torture, ritualistic cannibalism, reanimation, reward after death, endless punishment after death, end of the world; all at once they worship it, welcome it, embrace it, praise it, instigate it and fear it. It pervades their scripture. Their shamans use it to instill fear and compliance in their children. Without death obsession as a foundational aspect of their belief, their religion would have little meaning and hold much less appeal to its adherents.

Christianity is little more than a cult of death worship. Moloch would be envious of these followers' death fixation. A more grotesque and pitiful mind disease is hard for a thinking person to imagine.

52

Atheist in a Foxhole: Hump's Exposure to Military "Christian Love"

25 Jul 2008

A friend sent me an article about the military's co-ercion of US soldiers to attend church. In brief, trainees at Fort Leonard Wood were being pres-sured to attend Baptist religious services, under the guise of it being an Army directed off-day activity. Anyone not submitting to the proselytizing "field day" was restricted to base and made to train.

It's not an isolated occurrence. The military is rife with Christian fanatics throughout the chain of com-mand. Recent stories in the news about the Air Force Academy's anti-Semitic activity and Christian proly-tizing caused a major investigation. An atheist soldier in Iraq is suing the Army for discriminating against his non-belief and receiving death threats from Christian soldiers for his rejection of their religious proselytiz-ing. The Army has even had instances of Evangelicals proselytizing to Iraqi civilians, in violation of military policy and against Iraqi law.

But this isn't a new phenomenon. I was personally on the receiving end of this kind of un-American, fanatical Christian mentality when I joined the Army in 1967. And I paid a price.

I'll skip over the details of what prompted a reasonably intelligent, suburban New Yorker from an upper middleclass family to leave college and set himself up to go to Vietnam. But, the bottom line is I left college and volunteered for the draft in the spring of '67. By October I was in basic training in Fort Jackson, South Carolina.

The initial introduction and indoctrination into the military is disorienting to say the least. You're perpetually being yelled at, verbally punished and physically pushed to the limit. You don't know up from down, your ass from a hole in the ground, and they make sure you're told that hourly. By the end of the first week the thought of having a day of rest was very appealing.

In formation outside the barracks that Saturday after the first week of basic, the drill sergeant, a Southern white trash "lifer" (career soldier) with the IQ of a sandbag, announced to the platoon that he expected 100% attendance at church the next morning. The directive was roundly answered with a loud "YES SERGEANT!" by my fellow trainees. My non-responsiveness caught his eye. Charging over to me, he pushed his skinny pock-marked sweating face as close as he could to mine. The exchange went something like this:

SGT. Cracker: *"What's your PROBLEM, Trainee?"*

Pvt. Hump: *"No problem Sergeant. I just won't be attending church tomorrow."*

SGT. Cracker: *"What the fuck you talking about, BOY?"*

Pvt. Hump: *"Well, Sergeant, I don't believe in a God. It would be a violation of my convictions to go to religious services."*

SGT. Cracker: *"You a fuckin ATHEIST, BOY?"* (The 'f' anointing my face with his spit)

Pvt. Hump: *"Yes, Sergeant, I guess I am."*

SGT. Cracker: *"Well, ain't that something special!? Tell ya what, if I don't have 100% attendance at church tomorrow, including your Godless New York shit ass, then the whole platoon will be confined to barracks for the day. Is that clear, PRIVATE?"*

Pvt. Hump: *"Sergeant, I thought one of the things we are fighting for is to preserve our freedoms. Don't I have the right, the freedom, not to go to church without penalizing me and everyone else?"*

SGT. Cracker: *"Right???!! Maybe your fellow soldiers can help convince you of what your RIGHTS are. IS THAT CLEAR TRAINEES?"*

In unison the platoon shouted back *"YES SERGEANT!"* and we were dismissed.

The dehumanization of the trainee experience tends to make fellow sufferers closer. It's part of the whole point of the process; building a combat force with oneness. So, I thought I had made some new and close comrades. I felt they would understand my position, even back me up against a bully and this injustice.

But, as we sat in the barracks, all that comradeship evaporated in the face of the sergeant's threat. This was the Army, and these were Christians, and I was, after all, *"the other."* There was one Jew, but he had been singled out on his first day. Nicknamed "CK" (Christ Killer) by the drill sergeants, and so abused by them, his religion so vilely defamed and insulted, that he demurred and opted to attend church with the

Christians. He'd had his fill of Christian love … it was my turn.

Over the next hour I was subjected to some serious peer pressure, verbal abuse and threats. I understood their frustration, but my perspective was totally lost on them. Finally, two guys jumped me and a fist fight ensued. One of the two was my "buddy".

The fight lasted about three minutes, a veritable eternity to me. After it was done, with fat lips and bloody noses all around, things calmed down. I reiterated my unchanged position. Everyone was resigned to our communal fate. I didn't sleep that night.

The next morning the platoon went to church, I went to KP, and everyone but me had the rest of the day off base. The bluff of the threat was called; the Sergeant opted not to pursue it further, or again. I went on to AIT (Advanced Infantry Training) at Ft. Polk, Louisiana; eventually ended up in Vietnam in April '68, as expected; and was assigned as a non-jump qualified ("leg") replacement to the 82nd Airborne as a rifleman "11 Bravo" where I was an atheist in a foxhole.

I learned three things from that experience at Ft. Jackson:

1) The military expects everyone to be Christian; to be other is to be less.

2) Standing up to the injustice of religious coercion makes you feel more like an American.

3) Christians are hypocrites to whom protecting freedom and rights means *their* freedom and *their* rights, not the rights of everyone.

And so it evidently continues forty years later.

53

The Fallacy of Prophecy Fulfillment: Why Can't Fundamentalists Get It?

29 Jul 2008

Likely all of us have heard Christians declare that there are some three hundred prophesies in the Tanakh, the Hebrew Bible, called by Christians the Old Testament (OT), that were fulfilled by Jesus and documented in the New Testament (NT). This is a foundational element of the Jesus as God and Messiah belief: Jesus fulfilled the old prophesies.

I have always tried to explain to these credulous folks that the NT is simply a sequel to the OT. That is, since the OT prophesies were known by the Jewish authors of the NT, how hard would it be to write a mythical account of the life of one Jesus to match and thus fulfill those early prophesies? I mean, how difficult can that be to understand? At least mull it over and consider its simplicity.

But they dismiss it at face. It's just too obvious, too simple and too worldly to be a viable explanation. It's easier, it seems, for them to accept a mystical magical complex supernaturalism for which there is zero evidence and no corroborating/repeatable examples, than to consider the simplest and most logical explanation for prophesy fulfillment. They cannot even understand the concept; it actually confuses them. Remarkable, peculiar and incredibly frustrating.

I just finished reading *Constantine's Sword* by James Carroll; ex Catholic priest, biblical scholar, Catholic Church historian, Christ follower. An excellent read, it was on the New York Times Best Seller List. I highly recommend it.   He explains the New Testament prophesy fulfillment bugaboo this way: It's not *"history prophesized,"* but simply multiple examples of *"prophesy historicized."* In other words, exactly what I have been explaining to the faithful sheep all along.

The NT writers took OT prophesy, known by every Jew, and applied it to Jesus 50-70 years after his death, as though it was a historical fact. It was done to imbue him with the mythical Jewish Messiah status. In so doing, the ancient Hebrew Bible would be "proof of" and "witness to", Jesus' Messiahship ... a great selling point if the intent was to recruit Jews to your new cult. And indeed, Christianity was originally an exclusively Jewish focused cult.

Carroll goes on to explain that Jesus' contemporary followers would never have conceived of this messiah status; it would have come as a complete shock to Jesus himself who would have likely considered it blasphemous.

"Prophesy historicized" is the concept I've been trying to describe to the sheeple for years. It took a liberal, thinking Catholic scholar to help me name it. Live and learn.

54

Let's Question the "Word of GOD;" the Theists Sure Won't

01 Aug 2008

The faithful say that the Bible is the Word of God. Some believe it was inspired by God, others (the more seriously damaged) believe it to be actually written by God Himself ... in long hand. Some believe God wrote it in English; those people usually reside in the deep South and are often married to close relatives.

Unlike 95% of Christians, I've read books on the origins of religious scripture written by biblical scholars, among them *Who Wrote the Bible,* by R.E. Freidman. He explains in great detail how various social imperatives and controls, and political infighting shaped the stories, lore, and laws of the Old Testament scripture. Scholars can even determine from which of the two divided kingdoms of Israel and Judea the authors came, and whether or not they were of the priestly class, all based on competing social and political emphasis, scriptural nuance and contradictory/competing text. It's fascinating.

That the Old Testament is full of cruel, homophobic, anti-feminist, pro-slavery, pro-rape, and pro-genocidal stories and laws that suborn them is old news. It's the stuff you read and shake your head over. But every now and then there is a passage that makes you just scratch your head in wonder. One that does it for me is this:

"Ye shall keep my statutes. Thou shalt not let thy cattle gender with a diverse kind: thou shalt not sow thy field with mingled seed: neither shall a garment mingled of linen and woolen come upon thee." Leviticus 19:19

Remember, that's GOD talking, and He's damn serious! The God whom theists believe created the universe and everything in it; who has existed forever; who is all knowing, all powerful – here He is giving His chosen people fashion tips and admonishing them not to create hybrid cattle or plants.

While inexplicably idiotic to you and me, Christian apologists are, by their infirmity, compelled to defend it as logical and possessing deep significance. Some of their explanations for Leviticus 19:19 are as follows:

"A pure breed of plant or animal is better than a mixed breed, and God knows this." "God established these laws to ensure that low quality fabrics are not produced."[1]

There are many other apologetics sites that provide the same or similar explanations.

So what are we to believe? God knowingly gives the Jews bad advice on animal husbandry and agriculture? That He didn't know cross breeding could increase

---

[1] http://www.thercg.org/questions/p185.a.html

milk and meat production, improve plant resistance to drought and pests, as well as increase the heartiness/adaptability of the species by incorporating the best qualities of other breeds? And what erroneous info led God to believe that garments made of fabric blends just don't hold up to His rigid standards of quality and performance?

Look, these weren't offhand suggestions – He meant business! Breaking ANY of God's laws was punishable by some pretty stiff penalties, up to and including being stoned to death. *["Hey Saul, that had better NOT be wool fringe I see on your cotton robe!"]*

So, one might wonder if these instructions were so important to God why is it that Christians wear wool blend clothes, and Christian farmers cross breed cattle and grow hybrid plants? Answer – the usual feeble reply: *"Oh...we don't have to follow the old laws since Jesus died for us."*

And yet, when asked, they can't begin to explain:

1. Why did God give bad animal husbandry/agricultural dictates to begin with?
2. Why would Jesus' death make the cross breeding of cattle and plants suddenly okay and in the best interest of his creations; and why would it render blending wool and plant fibers in a garment acceptable? How does the death of a Jew suddenly made those fabrics last longer?
3. Finally, how come God has a bug up His butt for these obscure laws, but neglected laws about prohibiting pedophilia, slavery and demanding women be treated equally with men?

Christians should wonder about those things but they don't and they won't. To do so could lead to thinking, which makes their heads hurt and might weaken their faith. Meanwhile, the rest of us will wonder how Christians can be so utterly simple minded, and their God such a numbskull.

[Note: The rabbinic/Jewish explanations are much more conventional and as you'd expect, logical, inferring they are a man made construct. It speaks to these laws as having been devised to honor God by not altering His original creations, and to protect the privileged/unique attire of the Priestly class who wore wool and linen during religious rites. *But, shush!!! ...don't tell the Christians.* Their explanations are so much more entertaining.]

55

Delusional Christians Shouldn't Be Allowed to Vote

04 Aug 2008

Yes, I know ... a very controversial and seemingly inflammatory statement; a position that certainly seems at odds with my strong defense of the Constitution and commitment to personal freedoms. But, before you throw this aside as some radical fascist concept, let's examine it dispassionately.

The Fifteenth Amendment to the Constitution says: *"The right of citizens of the United States to vote shall not be denied or abridged by the United States or by any State on account of race, color, or previous condition of servitude."*

Note that it doesn't say anything about people who are so deluded, or who have such low IQs, that their ability to exercise their franchise in a logical and informed manner is rendered nil. In fact, certain conditions can and do bar people from voting. Convicted felons can't vote, and in many states the insane, severely retarded, and mentally incompetent are prohibited from voting. For instance, New Jersey's Constitution forbids an *"idiot or insane person"* from voting. Thus, voting is a privilege that can be lost and not an unconditional "right." So, with that as precedence let's define the "delusional Christian" conditions that I propose should negate a persons voting privilege.

First, let me be clear – I am <u>not</u> suggesting that simple belief in God, Jesus as God, the Trinity, prayer, miracles, dead rising, transubstantiation, heaven, hell, etc,. etc., the normal Christian doctrine, should disqualify a person from being able to vote. And I'm not suggesting that refusal to accept certain sexual practices, social behaviors, or a woman's right to reproductive freedom because of a religious conviction is delusional. These things are just symptomatic of the stubborn denial of reality and modernity caused by the brain's religion meme. I'm talking about those people who are so far gone, their minds so infected by religious infirmity, that their ability to discern reality from delusion is impeded. For instance:

People who, in spite of overwhelming, irrefutable, scientific evidence believe the Earth is less than 10,000 years old because the Bible tells them so ... are incapable of rational discernment.

People who believe that God talks to them, that angels visit them and who claim to have seen witches, devils and demons ... are not mentally equipped to participate in the choosing of our nation's leaders.

People who are convinced that 9/11, hurricane Katrina, the collapse of a bridge in Minnesota, the death of US soldiers, the spread of AIDS, etc., is God's divine punishment for society's acceptance of homosexuality ... lack the rational thought necessary to evaluate real world decisions.

People who burn Harry Potter books; who believe magic/"witchcraft" is real and inspired by Satan; who conduct exorcisms on unwilling victims; who are, unbeknownst to them, one step away from ingesting or dispensing cyanide laced Kool-Aid ...are thus ill-equipped to exercise the voting privilege.

Let's face it. It's bad enough that theists are so credulous and gullible that they will believe most anything the Bible, their clergy, or a right wing candidate feeds them. The last thing we need is to allow the most irrational fringe element of their kind to make decisions that can shape our future. If we are destined to screw ourselves by electing the wrong candidates, let the error be on the heads of people who can at least approach clear and reasoned thought unencumbered by schizophrenia-induced hyper-religiosity.

56

Defining "True" Christians

09 Aug 2008

"Christianity teaches people to be kind and peaceful and loving. Anyone who does evil acts certainly isn't acting in a loving manner; therefore they can't really be a TRUE Christian no matter what they say."

How many times in discourse with Christians have you heard this, or something similar? It is the quintessential example of the "No True Scotsman" fallacy.

I've always found entertaining Christian declarations of who amongst their fellow Jesus worshippers are or aren't "True Christians." I have seen fundamentalists call Catholics "Satan worshippers" and "Idolaters;" the Pope "The Anti-Christ;" and declare their brethren in less fanatical protestant sects "unsaved." I've witnessed so-called loving Christians call Mormons "heathens" at worst, and "cultists" at best (I don't disagree, after all aren't all religions cults?)

Certainly, most of the 2,800+/- Christian sects disdain and deny the flavor of Christianity the Jehovah's

Witnesses' practice for their rejection of the non-Biblical concept of Trinity. In fact the level of disgust "mainstream Christians" have for JWs is almost as epic as their infamous scorn for Jews.

And how many of us have pointed to the astounding number of documented child molesting, thieving and manipulative priests, ministers, parsons, pastors, church administrators, church youth leaders and exposed televangelists, only to have the self-righteous, self-appointed determiners of qualification declare them "not True Christians?"

Finally, there is the not-so-occasional religious homicidal maniac, like the church going anthrax scientist who recently committed suicide, or the child killing mother in the throes of religious fanatic delusion – all dismissed as "not True Christians." How very convenient, and self-serving.

Evidently the litmus test to be a "True Christian" isn't as simple as being baptized and believing in Jesus as savior (as the New Testament says). Nope. It seems to necessitate belonging to the same sect, having the same dogma/rituals, and holding the preferred position on social issues like abortion or homosexual marriage. Or if mentally unstable, at least manifest the same instability/share the same psychosis as the judgmental Christians self appointed to determine who is and isn't a "True Christian."

And should one Christian's actions cause embarrassment or place fellow Christians in a bad light…oh, well… that's the "not True Christian" kiss of death. This in spite of the doctrine that says one is not condemned by bad acts, nor saved by good acts or good deeds, simply by acceptance of Jesus as The Savior.

So what drives this need to disown their own out of hand? Two things:

1. To be a member of one of those "other cults," or to have alternate positions on social issues, threatens the mainstream Christian flock members' certainty of the validity of their own sect and positions.

2. Christians who embarrass other faithful by their unsavory/illegal acts even when done at the alleged direction of Jesus, casts all Christians in a bad light and undercuts the credibility of the "True" Christians (as if Christianity had any credibility to begin with).

If you tell me you don't believe in God(s) I promise I won't question your "True atheism"... even if you are a pervert, anti-choice, send anthrax letters, and/or vote Republican.

57

BLASPHEMY!! Fun for the Whole Family

12 Aug 2008

The American Heritage Dictionary defines blasphemy as:
- *A contemptuous or profane act, utterance, or writing concerning God or a sacred entity; The act of claiming for oneself the attributes and rights of God.*

I define blasphemy as a fun past time when performed in the presence of easily offended theists.

In the US, a number of states still have blasphemy laws on their books, even though in 1952 the Supreme Court negated them by declaring New York State's blasphemy law illegal since it preempts free speech and violates the First Amendment of the Constitution. There has been no successful prosecution of a blasphemer anywhere in the US since 1928. That guy, an atheist and Evolution advocate, was fined $25 by the state of Arkansas (no surprise there).

Massachusetts' blasphemy law is a sterling example of theists' delusional need to protect their supreme being's sensibilities. It goes back to the early 18th century, is still on the books and is particularly onerous:

"Whoever willfully blasphemes the holy name of God by denying, cursing or contumeliously reproaching God, His creation, government or final judging of the world, or by cursing or contumeliously reaching Jesus Christ or the Holy Ghost, or by cursing or contumeliously reproaching or exposing to contempt and ridicule, the holy word of God contained in the holy scriptures shall be punished by imprisonment in jail for not more than one year or by a fine of not more than three hundred dollars, and may also be bound to good behavior."

Three hundred dollars back then wasn't chicken feed, and the prison conditions left much to be desired. Simply declaring that you deny the existence of God was blasphemy. Never mind calling Jesus gay, publishing pictures of Jesus in less than a flattering light, or laughing out loud at the contradictions and idiocy of the Bible.

Is it any wonder that atheists were in no hurry to come out of the closet, much less write "Ye Olde Atheist Blog" and hand them out on Sundays?

Well, times have changed a lot. But there are still God-Fearing-Bible Banging-Tongue Talking-Reality Denying- Re-Birthed Christians who would absolutely LOVE to get those laws enforced. And guess what … they practically can.

Many US institutions and even some governmental and quasi-governmental authorities have written "Hate Speech" prohibitions into their codes of conduct. There are hate speech polices in some state universities, even though it is recognized as a violation of the First Amendment. While intended to quash anti-Semitic, anti-gay, or anti-minority rhetoric which could ignite hostility, it's a short step from there to some fanatical born again Christian nut case demanding a college's Freethinkers Club be disbanded, or an atheist sticker be removed from a private car because it's offensive to their beliefs.

It hasn't happened yet, but it's only a matter of time. When it does happen my response will be exactly what every Free Thinking person's should be: *"To hell with you, and the man-god you rode in on."*

58

"Where was God?"

16 Aug 2008

"*W* here was God?*"* That was the MSNBC online World News headline on a story about the refugees from war-torn Georgia fleeing to Russia. Here's the quote:

"Mother Nonna said she had never seen so many terrified children clinging to their mothers' skirts. The most difficult thing was to answer their question: 'Where was God? she said. They had so much fear in their eyes."

Ever since man created God in his image that question has been asked. After every act of man's inhumanity to man; after every earthquake, famine, flood, typhoon; during every pandemic believers have pondered that question. For after all, if their god can see and feel their suffering, hear their screams and pleas, and yet do nothing, what possible use is the god they created and to whom they spent so many hours praying, worshipping, and praising?

Then follow the escape clauses and apologetics from the faithful and their shamans:

"Evil is the work of Satan, not God." Thus, Satan is more powerful than God? Or Satan is working with God's approval? And if it was not the work of God how then this?:

"I form the light, and create darkness: **I make peace, and create evil:** *I the LORD do all these things."* Isaiah 45:7. God clearly takes credit for His evil creating ways.

"It is God's wrath for man's sinful ways." Wouldn't a warning like a flaming sword in the sky, or an army of angels hovering over the UN while broadcasting live on TV have had the same attention-getting effect, while sparing thousands or millions of innocent lives, along with the lives of potentially repentant sinners? Wouldn't THAT be the action of a "loving God" for His creations?

"Its part of God's plan that we can't possibly know or understand." What kind of merciful loving god includes in its "plan" the horrific deaths of thousands of children with AIDS? Or the incineration of innocent people asleep in their village in Iraq, Darfur or Georgia? Or the hideous deaths of those who jumped to their doom from the top of the World Trade Towers to avoid the flames? "Plan?" The plan of a psychotic god.

When you cut though all the inventive excuses, all the platitudes that they have been carefully taught to fend off doubt and ensure their mind slavery, it always comes back to that old philosophical paradox, I paraphrase Epicurus:

Is God able to stop/prevent these evil things, but unwilling, thus malevolent?

Or is God not able to stop these things, thus impotent?

If God is neither willing nor able, then why call him God?

The answer to that paradox, and to the "Where was God?" question that has been on the lips of refugees for millennia is the same, and found in none of the above. The answer, its lesson, is just now a glimmer of recognition in the minds of some percentage of those Georgian refugees whose reasoning has been stirred awake. It is a lesson hard learned.

Welcome to reality.

59

Political Whores Pay Homage to the Religious Right

17 Aug 2008

They came hat in hand, groveling, paying homage to a religious icon; courting the flock he herds, professing their religiosity, their "family values," and their piety.

On Saturday, August 16th, 2008 John McCain and Barack Obama were summoned by the Grand Inquisitor of the Evangelical mind slaves, Rick Warren. They stood before him to assure him and his pod people that they are seriously concerned about what women do with their uteruses. They professed their horror for homosexual marriage, declared their love of a mythical man-god, quoted scripture, and all but stuffed their mealy-mouths with communion wafers and skinny dipped in the baptismal font.

This is what candidates for the leadership of the most powerful nation on the planet have come to. This is to what they have descended.

- ➢ While a useless war drags on for its fifth year and young kids die for a sand pit that is destined to become a Muslim theocracy;

- ➢ while Afghanistan lapses back into turmoil as the Taliban surges;

- ➢ while our unemployment rate goes up, business declines, and jobs are exported;

- ➢ while our airlines are on the verge of collapse;

- ➢ while foreign businesses buy up iconic American corporations;

- ➢ while China's economy grows at three to five times that of the US's;

- ➢ while property values drop and home foreclosures reach record highs;

- ➢ while food, gasoline and heating oil costs suck people dry;

- ➢ while we have 60% dependency on foreign oil, and invest in no new domestic sources;

- ➢ while our military is depleted and impotent to defend us in the event of a real threat;

- ➢ while our educational system lags behind virtually every other industrialized nation;

- ➢ while our bridges and infrastructure rot;

- ➢ while our deficit hits a record $400+ billion;

- ➢ while our national debt reaches $9 trillion, the highest percentage of our GDP in 16 years;

- ➢ while the disparity between rich and middleclass incomes widen;

- ➢ while healthcare costs rise annually beyond the reach of many;

➢ while Social Security is poised to self destruct in 9 years;

➢ while our unsecured borders permit millions of illegals to enter our country at will;

➢ while our Homeland Security technology has yet to reach needed levels;

➢ while the need for alternative energy screams for aggressive action and incentives;

➢ while our national prestige, influence and credibility evaporates;

like a couple of whores vying for a trick's business, these two sycophants addressed the really critically important elements in the minds of Evangelical Christians:

➢ **will they allow humans with matching genitalia to marry each other?**

➢ **will they ensure control over women's uteruses?**

➢ **when does life begin?**

➢ **which one of them loves Jesus more?**

And why? To placate and woo the votes of religious zombies who still think a giant celestial bogeyman created the universe in six days and who seek to subordinate the freedoms of those not encumbered with their religious doctrine.

What next?? Meetings with the UFO nuts, and alien abductees? With Young Earthers, and Bigfoot enthusiasts? Will they now kowtow to the Ken Ham Creationists and Intelligent Design whackos, the 9/11 conspiracy neurotics, the "Elvis is alive and living in Phoenix" crazies, the "Moon Landing was a Fake" psychos? They may as well, and promise them all of their support and convince them that they share their mental infirmities to one degree or another. Hell, after all, the Presidency is at stake.

This is what our political process has come to. This is where candidates focus their campaign. These are the issues upon which Americans decide the fate of their nation. If the old canard *"We get the government we deserve"* is true, bend over and kiss America's ass goodbye.

60

God and Little League

23 Aug 2008

I'm watching the Little League World Series, Louisiana versus Hawaii. Louisiana is having their butts handed to them in the last inning, having already blown a four run lead. Hawaii has opened a can of whup-ass on them.

As the camera pans the bleachers I catch a glimpse of a man, the father of a Louisiana player based on his LSU cap, holding up a white board upon which, printed in block letters, is this:

"With GOD all things are POSSIBLE!!"

I ponder this for a moment. Even though I know that Louisiana is a hotbed of religious affliction, I am taken aback. What is this religious dad telling his kid exactly? That if he believes in God hard enough, that God will influence the game? That God will give him improved hand-eye coordination, inspire him to extra speed and bless him with base running smarts that he may better vanquish the opposing twelve-year-old foes?

Is he telling his kid that God will favor his team, and help defeat the presumably less devout/godless Hawaiians? Is he saying that God is tuned into the game and might be willing to take sides, thus pray to influence God's support?

Is his guidance to focus on Jesus and just let "the force" guide him? Can it be he is saying that the coach's strategy, the teamwork and his own son's skill are less than, or equally important, to the outcome of the game as is God's divine intervention? That perhaps in spite of his son's inadequacy or his teams lesser talents, not to worry... God is on your side?

It's hard to know what goes through the minds of the religiously afflicted. The very fact that this dad needs to drag a deity into his kid's ballgame is creepy enough for me.

Here's the good news: Hawaii won it 7-5. Maybe the sign should have read: *"With GOD all things are POSSIBLE – but don't hold your breath!"*

Hawaii – 1
God – 0

61
Gay Jesus
27 Aug 2008

In an atheist blog where I am a frequent participant, the owner posted an article about a college atheist group which created a poster depicting Jesus in a gay relationship.

The atheist blogger was incensed and decried the atheist students' insensitivity. His readers' comments, atheists all, were similarly indignant:

"It is meant simply to offend, it doesn't open dialog!"

"It's childish and does the 'cause' no good."

"We'll never win converts by offending them. It's an ineffective tactic!"

How remarkably shortsighted. How peculiarly unsophisticated is their perspective. How completely they miss the point. My take is entirely different. The gay image of Jesus DOES provoke dialogue; IS an effective tactic; its perceived offensiveness has a purpose, and conversion isn't it.

Consider this -- Christians have promulgated anti-Semitism for almost 1,800 years. Yet they disregard, forget, or ignore the fact that Jesus was himself a Jew. His teachings were directed toward fellow Jews, not gentiles, as a Jewish reform movement. Gentile conversions were an afterthought, thanks to Paul. The demonization of Jews was subsequently embedded in their scripture by the biblical authors, and not attributable to Jesus. I would guess that Jesus would be disgusted by that.

Similarly, Christians habitually overlook Jesus' teaching of *"Judge not, lest ye be judged."* They condemn homosexuality and extend that condemnation to acts of exclusionism, bigotry, incivility, even violence toward homosexuals. Jesus never said to do that. Indeed, if he will accept and defend an adulteress and prostitute, logic says he would likely do the same for a homosexual, even though both adultery and homosexuality were punishable by death per the Hebrew Bible.

Jesus was alleged to have been in his early thirties, referred to as "rabbi," traveled with twelve men, and was unmarried. In the Jewish tradition an unmarried rabbi in his thirties is virtually unheard of. Additionally, there are some scriptural references that seem to hint at a very special relationship with one of his apostles. Many theologians and lay biblical scholars have speculated as to Jesus' possible homosexuality. There is no incontrovertible evidence pro or con.

But, if he had emotions, if he ate, if he drank, if he urinated and defecated then it's entirely possible he had sexual feelings too. Thus, speculation as to his sexual proclivities is valid. If modern statistics mean anything, there was a 1 in 10 chance he was gay, assuming he existed at all. It may not suit the Christian sensibilities to think that way, but there it is ... deal with it.

That Jesus might have been gay doesn't make him an evil person and doesn't discredit his teachings. Why should it matter? That it matters to Christians or uncritically thinking atheists – that they see a gay portrayal of Jesus as an evil – is precisely the point of that student group's poster. We live in the 21st century. We know sexual preference is genetically determined. A person should no more be condemned for being gay as for being bald, black, or short. It shouldn't be perceived as evil. If Jesus were gay it shouldn't negate his status, or subject him, or anyone, to abuse any more than Jesus' being Jewish would justify anti-Semitic vitriol against him or anyone (as his followers have so enthusiastically done to Jews for two millennia).

That gay Jesus poster instigates this discussion. It disturbs and shocks the status quo. It is a valid in-your-face attempt by a put upon minority to get Christians to think more broadly, more modernly, with more tolerance. They don't have to like it, it just has to stimulate thought. It does that, even among the unthinking.

The fact that some people, especially atheists, perceive the "Jesus as gay" portrayal as unjustifiable provocation, leads me to wonder if they themselves are homophobic. Or is it that they are simply saying its okay for only Christians to be homophobes?

Why should it be so?

62

Christian Speak Translated Here

01 Sep 2008

It's just after three PM on Labor Day. I'm listening to a report about hurricane Gustav on NPR. The commentator is phone interviewing hurricane evacuees from Mississippi, areas of which are being hit harder than New Orleans.

One woman proudly explains in an upbeat voice steeped in a southern accent:

*"Well, looks like my house is under water. They say it crested at over 16 feet, and my house is at 16 feet. But I'm used to it. I lost a house to a hurricane five years ago, lost my second house to Katrina, now losing this one. **But I'm not worried, God takes care of everything.**"*

To those who aren't versed in Christian Speak, this probably sounds confusing. One would not be mistaken to conclude that a number of things are very, very wrong with that woman's thinking. For instance, one might think:

"Hey, imbecile, maybe you should stop rebuilding your hovel in a flood zone.";

or

"God's been trying to take care of everything alright, but you keep escaping anyway.";

or

"Has it occurred to you that if a God existed who gave a fiddlers damn about you He'd stop screwing over you and your continuously flooded brethren in the first place?"

To those of us who have studied Christian Speak here's what *"God takes care of everything"* actually means: It means that she has Federal Flood Insurance, for which she pays nothing or next to nothing because of her poverty/low income status. It's funded by taxpayers who will bear the cost to rebuild her home and replace its furnishings with very little out of pocket expense to the homeowner herself. So, what does she care if she gets a new home every three to five years as long as the government is stupid enough to keep throwing good money after bad?

You might say: *"But that's got nothing to do with God or the supernatural"* and you'd be correct of course. But to Christians whose minds cannot make a distinction between supernatural intervention and the reality of taxation and misguided mismanaged governmental programs, every handout, every avoidance of having to bear the brunt of financial disaster themselves, means GOD has worked His miracle. GOD has intervened. GOD takes care of everything.

The bureaucrats who will assess her loss, write the check, and hand her our tax dollars are simply agents of God; angels who will lift this woman from her homelessness to her newly built government funded house. And she won't thank you or I for building her new abode and comfort. Her imaginary sky buddy will get the credit. Hallelujah Sister!!!

Christian Speak – a marvelous invention of the self-deluded. Just slightly more annoying than talking in tongues.

63

Faith Healers: The Ultimate Testament to Christian Delusion

07 Sep 2008

D o an internet search for "faith healers" and you'll
get to watch YouTube videos of the most despicable and bizarre acts of cruelty and deception
on the face of the planet.

Diabetics, children with spina bifida, wheelchair
bound paralytic elderly, people with practically every
known malady come to these revivals desperate for
a chance to have some self-proclaimed agent of God
heal them, where medical science could not. They
come hoping that their faith in God, and faith in this
man who claims to be the conduit for God's healing
power, will make them whole, will resurrect their dead
organs, their disintegrated nerve cells, and their wast-
ing muscle tissue.

Of course, time permits only a very few to be selected to receive a face-to-face laying on of hands by
this agent of Jesus. Some are employed shills who will
invariably collapse to the floor upon the electric touch

of the healer, jump up, claim to be healed, praise the Lord and fade immediately into obscurity, never to be seen again; their names and medical histories forever unavailable and lost to posterity. How convenient.

So many others, the truly ill and incurable, are used as just so many pawns. They stand or sit there expectantly, with the hands of the healer working their magic, his voice rising and exhorting the Lord to HEAL. Then the candidate faces a dilemma. They are challenged by the thousands of eyes of the faithfully expectant, as to whether or not they felt the power of God enter their bodies through the slap to their forehead, or a kick to their chest. The afflicted person's options are two fold: *"YES, Thank You JESUS!!"* and be praised by the frenzied multitudes, be the focus of their hallelujahs, prayers and waving of hands by their fellow sheep; or say "NO" and be dismissed as lacking faith and given the bums rush from the stage to clear the way for the next act. There are genuine and immediate benefits to saying yes.

And yet, whenever those claiming to have been healed can be found by skeptics and debunkers, invariably there are two outcomes: Either the perfectly healthy person can produce no medical records or genuine accredited physicians who will attest to their original illness; or the person is still in their wheelchair, still paralyzed, still succumbing to their disease.

None of this is a new revelation. All of it has been documented by debunkers and the media for years. Faith healers are exposed regularly for their tricks and accomplices in the audience, for their less than holy lifestyles and illegal money making schemes. The Benny Hinns, the Todd Bentleys, the Peter Popovs, the

Theodore Wolmarans, the W.V Grants, the list of the disgraced and exposed is legion.

And yet the gullible faithful keep coming, they keep believing, they keep trusting and tithing. Every newly anointed healer, with their promise of having a divine gift brings the bleating flocks of the desperate ready, willing and eager to be duped and sheared. Even those who were wheeled onto that stage and had their heads touched but who, sometimes after a brief improvement due to the placebo effect, find themselves still succumbing to their illnesses, still suffering, even <u>they</u> retain their belief that something good has or will eventually happen. There seems to be nothing that can shake them from their self-deception and involuntary servitude to religious delusion.

While my reasoning side tells me to despise these sheep for their ignorance, gullibility, credulity and blind denial of reality, more so even than the charlatans who prey upon them my – what shall I call it – humanity? makes me just pity them. Not for the incurable illness of their bodies, but for the incurable illness of the mind that is the religious virus.

64

Why do Some Christians Endorse Tyranny? Thank St. Paul

11 Sep 2008

Nothing speaks more of Saul of Tarsus', aka St. Paul's, credulity, blind stupidity, and rejection of reality, or his sycophantic kowtowing to Roman authority to win favor, than his own writings. This one is classic:

Romans

13:1 *Let every soul be subject unto the higher powers. For there is no power but of God:* **the powers that be are ordained of God.**

13:2 **Whosoever therefore resisteth the power, resisteth the ordinance of God: and they that resist shall receive to themselves damnation**

13:3 **For rulers are not a terror to good works, but to the evil. Wilt thou then not be afraid of the power?** *Do that which is good, and thou shalt have praise of the same.*

Understand what Paul is saying here: Rulers of countries are selected by God. Governments do not act against good people; they only act against citizens who are evil. Thus, never fear the power; do not resist the governing power, to do so means damnation in hell for opposing God's ordained earthly rulers.

In effect he was saying tyranny does not exist. And yet, if history has taught us anything it's that a people's own rulers have committed the most hideous acts against their most innocent citizens. A few notable examples among many:

The Spanish Inquisition

The extermination of the French Cathars

Russian pogroms against the Jews

Stalin's "purge", deportations and starvation of his own Soviet countrymen

Nazi Germany's "Final Solution," The Holocaust

Pol Pot's murder of 25% of his fellow Cambodians

Sudan's ethnic cleansing in Darfur

Extermination of Muslims by Christian Serbs in Kosovo

Those leaders were *"ordained of God?"* Those rulers did not commit *"terror to good works" [the innocent]?* The millions of victims of these governments had no reason to be *"afraid of the power?"* And it was, or would have been, wrong for these people to *"resist the power?"*

I doubt one out of one hundred moderate or liberal Christians are even aware of these verses. Of those few who have actually read the Bible most probably had no idea what Paul was saying, and just flew over it. But the Evangelical Christian Right fundies buy into it, endorse it 100%.

So, the next time you hear a Right Wing fundamentalist Christian say:

"You shouldn't fear uncontrolled governmental wire taps, questionable search and seizure, arbitrary access to your library book withdrawals, unhindered invasion of your internet

activity,   Unless you are an evildoer and have something to hide!" Remember from whom these bleating sheep got their mindless acceptance of God-endorsed tyranny. From a Roman sycophant named Paul who insisted government leaders are divinely empowered, would never act against you if you're innocent and must never be resisted.

One can only wonder if Paul rethought his position just before Nero had his empty head cut off.

Can an Atheist Vote Republican in the 21st Century?

17 Sep 2008

John McCain's 2001 abhorrence of the Religious Right's polices, politics, their objective to insert religion into our lives, our constitution and our government, is a thing of the past. Now he embraces them. His selection of a charismatic fundamentalist VP who believes in Creationism, insists only "abstinence" be taught to school children, is anti-abortion, anti-gay rights and who perceives this to be a Christian Nation is proof of that. It was a cynical ploy to cement Christian fundies' allegiance and rally their enthusiasm. McCain sold his soul to the Religious Right in an effort to get elected.

Rudolph Giuliani, when he was running for the Republican nomination, declared openly that if elected he would appoint Supreme Court judges in the same mould as Scalia, Thomas, Alito and Roberts; the most conservative and religious members of the Court. Justices who have in the past made their pro-religion sympathies clear. Scalia's ultra-religious views are just scary. Scalia said:

"The reaction of people of faith to this tendency of democracy to obscure the divine authority behind government should not be resignation to it, but the resolution to combat it as effectively as possible...". [1]

If those aren't the words of someone who suborns theocracy, I don't know what is.

The next president will be appointing between one and three Supreme Court Justices. Those appointees will determine the tilt of the court for many years to come. Whether governmental secularism will be sustained and personal freedoms retained, or whether the majority will seek to infuse more religion into our government, and truncate freedoms and equality by the guidance of a supreme being is at stake.

Let's make this real simple. The Republican Party is beholding to, if not run by, the Religious Right. It's the United States' version of the radical Islamic Hezbollah "Party of God." Its grasp on the Republican Party has not been loosened in spite of their loss of the House and Senate to the Democratic Party two years ago. The religious extremists' sole objective is to enforce their view of Christian "values," increase religiosity and return this country to the fictional Christian Nation that it never was. It was realization of this that resulted in my leaving the Republican Party after almost forty years. I am still a fiscal conservative, still pro Second Amendment, still favor a strong military and small government. But my commitment to a society free from theocratic control and stopping the

[1] http://www.nytimes.com/2002/07/08/opinion/from-justice-scalia-a-chilling-vision-of-religion-s-authority-in-america.html?scp=6&sq=religion&st=cse

blurring of the lines between church and state must take precedence.

Any Free Thinker activist who values our secular state; endorses equality and non-discrimination; and deplores the creeping religiosity that has invaded this country since the 50's, and which has been intensified during the eight long years of the Bush administration, cannot in good conscience vote Republican.

> If you agree that the government should have no say in who can marry;

> If you agree that "abstinence only" sex education shouldn't be government funded;

> If you agree the government shouldn't be deciding what books should or should not be in libraries, or what you can and cannot view on the internet;

> If you agree women should have complete control of their reproductive rights;

> If you agree that family alone should determine, with their physician, when their brain dead/terminally ill loved one should be allowed to die without government intrusion;

> If you agree that homosexuality isn't a choice but a genetic variation that shouldn't be punishable by second class citizenship;

> If you agree that religious symbolism in our public schools, government buildings, public property, or state license plates is a violation of the Constitution;

> If you agree biblical precepts have no place in determining our laws; that they should be

guided by secular ethics, and society's evolving morality;

➤ If you agree that teaching Creationism/Intelligent Design in public schools as an alternative "science" to evolutionary theory is detrimental to our youth's intellectual advancement;

➤ If you agree that pastors who use the pulpit to overtly support a political candidate or party should lose their tax exemption;

➤ If you agree that belief in a god should not be a prerequisite to holding public office;

Then voting Republican is counter to your ethics, philosophy, and conscience.   But, if you agree with George H.W. Bush that *"Atheists aren't patriots, and maybe not even Americans."* then voting Republican is exactly the right thing to do.

"Atheist Republican" is oxymoronic. It makes as much sense as a 1930's German "Jewish National Socialist".

66

"It Takes More Faith NOT to Believe in God."

21 Sep 2008

If you've never had a fundie, throw that phrase at you, you simply haven't been hanging around the religiously impaired enough. It's one of those platitudes, a catchy feel good phrase they pick up on the internet. They like to think of it as the "Rubik's Cube" of challenges ... a real brain teaser.

The technique is fallacy at face. They use a theological term, "faith", and try to apply it to the scientific method, the need for objective evidence, which is embraced by atheists and is devoid of blind faith. Faith by definition is *belief in the absence of solid evidence.* Therefore evidence is the antithesis of faith, the opposite. They are like matter and anti-matter – they simply cannot occupy the same space (not if one is intellectually honest). Thus, the statement is an exercise in the absurd.

There is overwhelming evidence that the Earth is very old as opposed to 6,000 to 10,000 years old as the biblical literalists believe; overwhelming evidence for evolution and none for Creation or an intelligent designer. Thus rejecting God(s) for an explanation for the species, or to reject a biblical timeline for Earth's age requires no faith at all. It's simply predicated on the lack of evidence. This isn't rocket science.

But, here's what eludes theists about this whole issue:

If we as atheists denied the concept of God simply as an arbitrary flat rejection, then indeed, it would be a decision predicated on faith. But, as thinking people, the rejection of a god concept is a result of accumulated evidence that supports natural causes for the universe. Not just one piece of evidence, not just one theory, but multiple theories with vast amounts of evidence.

Since cumulatively these natural pieces of evidence contradict supernatural explanations that are devoid of evidence, it requires no "faith" to accept the natural explanation and reject the supernatural explanation. From there it's a short step to testing and observing the ineffectiveness of prayer; the dearth of evidence for miracles, or reanimation of the dead, etc. Pretty soon, without any agenda to defend, the illogic of God and supernaturalism becomes self evident.

That they can't fathom this simple reasoning, and thus keep rolling out the "it takes more faith not to believe" canard, I attribute to theistic mental block, or simply to their desire to come up with a witty defense of their theism in the absence of evidence. It fails miserably in either case.

Science and reason neither demand nor require faith, only examination of the data, the evidence, without an agenda. Belief demands rejection/ignoring of any data/evidence to keep it viable, which is precisely what theists must do to keep their faith.

67

Piety & Politics **a Must Read**

25 Sep 2008

The Reverend Barry W. Lynn is the Executive Director of Americans United for Separation of Church and State. He is a devout and liberal follower of Christ, an ordained and practicing minister of the United Church of Christ and an attorney. Reverend Lynn has been an activist leading the charge against religious incursion into our government and our personal freedoms for many years. Americans United (AU) has successfully challenged the Religious Right's fanatic attempts to Christianize our country time and time again.

I recently read Rev. Lynn's book *Piety & Politics: The Right-Wing Assault on Religious Freedom*. His grasp of our history, the Constitution and the dangers of mixing religion and government is both educational and heartening to hear, especially from a clergyman. He doesn't hesitate to openly chastise those bastions of the Religious Right who falsely promote the fallacy that our laws were derived from Christian or biblical precepts, or that this is a "Christian Nation." This man stands at the top of my list of truth tellers, modern patriots and defenders of our freedoms. That he is himself a theist single-handedly changed my perspective about theists in general.

The following is a letter I wrote to Reverend Lynn. It should serve as a strong recommendation to read this important work.

Dear Rev. Lynn:

I just read Piety & Politics and wanted to say "thank you." I just said it by joining Americans United for Separation of Church and State moments ago, but I wanted to express it to you personally.

As an atheist I all too often fall into the trap of painting all Christians with the brush of Bible thumping religious fanatics. People who, in spite of my Vietnam service, Bronze Star, and Army Commendation medals, perceive me to be "… non-patriotic, perhaps not even an American" as George Bush Sr. once said, simply because I reject "belief."

People who would happily force every school to promote organized prayer, control women's reproductive rights, intervene in family decisions of when the terminally ill should be allowed to die, impose their biblical interpretations upon our secular Constitution and subjugate anyone whose sexual preference, personal philosophy, or religious views do not parallel theirs.

I know that the people of whom I speak aren't the majority of Christians, but I need to be reminded of that from time to time. Thanks for reminding me, and thanks for helping preserve America's freedoms from those who would truncate them.

I encourage every defender of the Constitution and advocate of the "wall of separation," theist or atheist, to buy this book and join Americans United.

68

The Miraculous Jesus Pill: Use Only as Directed

30 Sep 2008

I doubt there is an atheist alive who hasn't heard a Christian attribute spontaneous healing, injury pain reduction, or their recovery from drug, alcohol, or pornography addiction to Jesus' direct involvement. I dare say that there are millions of believers who will likewise attest to their God's healing power.

Not all of these testimonials are lies or even delusion. In fact, it's likely that a great many of the claims are actually being truthfully attested to by the devout believer. How is this possible?

"The placebo effect or placebo response is a therapeutic or healing effect of an inert medicine or ineffective therapy … due to the individual expecting or believing that it will work. **The placebo effect occurs when a patient is treated in conjunction with the suggestion from an authority figure or from acquired information that the treatment will aid in healing and the patient's condition improves."**[1]

---

[1] http://en.wikipedia.org/wiki/Placebo

Whether it's a sugar pill given by a medical authority, a monkey paw talisman given by a witch doctor, or a minister's suggestion of divine intervention by murmuring a prescribed prayer, the power of placebo is undeniable and observable. What science doesn't fully understand is how the mechanism actually works.

Unfortunately, unlike sugar pills, there is an addictive element to the Jesus Placebo. Once a beneficiary of that effect believes that all their ills, pains, tribulations, personal weaknesses and failures can be overcome by the Jesus pill, they become addicted to it. That addiction is manifested by increased dependency on the supernatural, and a corresponding devaluation of their own ability, own self worth, own strength, and own accountability for their lives and future. i.e. *"I couldn't have overcome my alcoholism with out Jesus! Maybe he'll get me a job now."*

And when the illness/pain/failure returns, as it invariably does, while a medical doctor or psychologist will explain to the patient the reason, and prescribe an effective medication and reality-based counsel, there isn't a shaman, a witch doctor, a minister, or a priest who will admit to the "patient" they were fed a faith placebo. Why should they? What possible benefit to the Church, to the retention of the faithful to the flock, could come from telling them the truth? So, instead of prescribing a double dose of reality they explain that the patient's faith was weak, and prescribe more and higher does of their religious placebo. *"Take two Jesus' and see me next Sunday."*

The mind is a wonderful thing. That religion messes with it so badly is akin to malpractice.

69

Social Gospel: Distorting the Scripture for Fun and Profit

03 Oct 2008

I've been hanging around Sojourner's website. It's one of those far left Christian sites that endorses redistribution of wealth (aka taxing people to death) to solve the planet's poverty problem. The philosophy they espouse is called "social gospel." It's headed by a leftist minister-author whose hybrid concept of capitalism and socialism has made him famous among far Left Liberation Christians.

It's different than most Christian blogs. It attracts a variety of Christians; those who see the site leader as some kind of prophetic cult figure, some normal liberal thinking Christians, a self-proclaimed "mystic" or two, an educated "non-theist Christian", and the usual Religious Right whackos. Here's the link if you want to check it out: http://www.sojo.net/blog/godspolitics/

But what's not different is that the vast majority of them, from the guest blog authors through the commenting readership, is that hardly any of them understand scripture or refuse to apply it truthfully.

Oh, they love to quote verse. They will cut and paste and paraphrase it endlessly to support the thread topic's political, social, or economic theme. The problem is it's never an accurate interpretation of the genuine meaning of the scripture they are quoting. NEVER! To them scripture is a tool to be adeptly manipulated to justify a far left social agenda ... with the blessing of Christ.

When their misapplication, or lack of understanding is pointed out, and their outright perversion of the verse to justify their argument is exposed, that's when the fun begins. The labored excuses, the denial, the protestations, the accusations of being disrespectful, the reinvention of context, the anger – it's remarkable to behold.

Take Paul's admonishment in 1 Timothy which says women are not to preach, and must be silent in church. At this site the verse is denied as a prohibition against women as pastors, and twisted as an endorsement that women *should* be ministers. Yep, you read that right. At least two people insisted that Paul didn't really mean what he said for *ALL* churches ... just Timothy's church. How did they get that interpretation? Where was the scriptural evidence, the inference, the source document? Nope, nada... they've got nothing. Why did the church fathers include 1Timothy in official canon if it was only for ONE church out of the hundreds? No answer... they just ignore and move on.

Another particularly vapid leftist Christian was bemoaning how the emergency "Wall Street Bailout" passed by congress will do nothing to spread the *"Good News of economic security that Jesus promised the poor."*

When I pointed out that the "Good News" Jesus spoke of had nothing to do with finance, but the spreading of the word of Jesus' coming, the good news of God, salvation, the Kingdom, etc., and that it was meant to lift the burden of heavy spirit from the poor, not the burden of their economic plight ... well, I may as well have been accused of being Satan himself.

The explanation of "good news" I provided is corroborated by every Christian biblical site on the web, and every knowledgeable biblical scholar. But, the corroborating documentation was of no importance to him. He refused to evaluate it. That there is zero reference to economic security or raising the poor from their financial plight, or governmental intervention in wealth redistribution to benefit the poor anywhere in scripture doesn't mean a thing to him. It didn't support his preferred socialist interpretation, thus why read and learn.

Basically what it comes down to is some combination of outright ignorance, or intentional distortion in order to support an agenda. Hey, if people have used the Bible to justify anything from slavery, to disenfranchising homosexuals, to anti-Semitism, to anti-Choice, why not distort it in support of confiscatory taxation to support the poor? And while you're at it, convince yourself you know what you're talking about.

Christian ignorance of scripture and their intellectual dishonesty is more than skin deep. It goes right down to the bone.

70
Pascal's Wager: I'll Take That Bet!

08 Oct 2008

Blaise Pascal, 17th century religious philosopher and mathematician, is famous for what is known as "Pascal's Wager." In short it posits that since the existence of God can neither be proven nor disproven, it is a better "wager" to believe than to not believe. The logic being that with belief you have nothing to lose. With disbelief, if God does exist, you're screwed for all time.

Naturally that logic only works if the possibility of a god existing happens to be the one god you pick to worship. Problem is, if a god existed it could well be one of the thousands and thousands of gods man has worshipped for time immemorial ... or even another god that man's mind has yet to conceive. Thus, if one picks a specific god to worship, the odds of <u>that god</u> being <u>the God</u>, the <u>correct god</u>, is from a mathematical perspective infinitesimally small.

So as opposed to having nothing to lose, a Christian may well find themselves confronting a god who is pissed as hell that his creation has been worshipping the wrong god and giving that wrong god all the credit throughout the theist's whole life. Homer Simpson figured it out when he said: *"But Marge, what if we are worshipping the wrong god. Every time we go to church we're just making him madder and madder."* Even Homer Simpson is right sometimes.

Then there's the good possibility (better than even odds, I say) that any such god being would be more sympathetic toward an atheist who opted to worship no god because there was no supporting evidence for any. If nothing else, atheism demonstrates the admirable quality of reason and logic that, presumably, this being would have wanted man to demonstrate seeing as how this god would have provided those attributes to man in the first place. In that scenario the godless heathen will be called "the first" in the Kingdom of Heaven (assuming this god offers a heaven thing).

Believe in God because you've got *"nothing to lose and everything to gain?"* Nothing to lose except your ability to reason and logic; your grasp on reality; a loss of self sufficiency; and conducting your life encumbered by an inane dogma, superstitious fears and intolerance for those who don't believe as you do. Nah, I'd take Pascal's wager, and give him 10 to 1 odds.

71

Letter from God to a Chosen Believer

15 Oct 2008

Dear Loyal Creation,

Hi! Hope things are going well for you. Of course, I already know how things are going; I'm just being congenially anthropomorphic for your benefit.

Hey, listen, before I go on I want to let you know I'm really sorry about your infant daughter dying. I wouldn't want you to think for one minute I didn't hear your prayers, and see your wife's tears as she sat by her bedside all those weeks and begged for me to save her. I'm sorry she had to suffer that slow agonizing death, but I haven't gotten around to providing the doctors with the formula and insight necessary to cure her condition. Maybe next week. I've been real busy trying to get the Cardinals into the playoffs.

Yes, I could have intervened and miraculously saved her, but I work in strange and mysterious ways, as I'm sure you've heard. Anyway, you can produce more offspring (shouldn't be too difficult for you, your wife is HOT! I'd do her myself, but the last time I did that it started a very messy cult). Oh, and thanks for not getting all pissy and giving up belief in me. I know I can count on your continued praise and worship. Hey, what else you got going for you in your life, right? Ha-ha ... just kidding! (Not really.)

Anyway, the reason I'm writing is to let you know you've been chosen to be my spokesperson on Earth. I know, I know, you're thinking *"What!? Me?? But I'm nobody, I'm not worthy!"* and you'd be right of course. I mean, I could pick someone with a much higher intellect, who possesses reasoning skills, and respects logic, say... an atheist. But, you know how they are. They'd ask for proof of my existence, evidence, and when I couldn't provide any, they'd know that they were having a delusion, go seek professional medical attention, and get back to the business of being normal productive people in short order. It just wouldn't work out.

You on the other hand are *so* credulous, *so* sheepishly faithful, *so* resistant to anything smacking of reality, *so* utterly deluded that I know can count on you to blindly mouth my orders and expectations for all mankind.

Right now you're thinking Pat Robertson already has that job. You're wrong. Pat's an asshat. I never communicate through him. In fact, it won't be long before he joins Jerry Falwell in that special place I created for so many of my beloved, but all-too-annoying creations. On the other hand, Fred Phelps does some consulting work for me on a pet project of mine, not the big stuff. Fred's a special guy.

So, here's the deal. Every so often I will communicate to you what I want you to tell the other sheep.

Sometimes it'll be through your dreams; sometimes as voices in your head; sometimes via your cell phone (I'll put you on my "Fav Five" speed dial). Occasionally, just for fun, I'll toss you a sign, sort of like those urine stains on men's room walls that look like Jesus, or the cheese sandwiches that look like that Mary chick. They don't mean anything, but you can have fun with it and supplement your income. God knows (hehehe) I mean, *I know* you could use the extra cash, given your career at Burger King isn't exactly destined for greatness.

Well, that's about it for now. Don't bother to show this letter to anyone; it's just a regular piece of notebook paper, blank except for the repetitive *"redruM, redruM"* scrawled in red crayon in your handwriting. People wouldn't understand.

I'll be in touch. Don't call me. I'll call you.

Omnisciently yours,

God

72

The Religious Right's Obsession with Your Morality Explained

23 Oct 2008

What's with the Far Right Christian obsession with other people's sexual behavior, reproduction and "morality?" In short: That they live by rules and "commandments" they believe are divinely established isn't enough. We must all abide by their concept of right and wrong or the shit will hit the fan for everyone.

Why? Because the all-knowing God thing sees everything that man does. He peeks into bedrooms; He evaluates your sexual practices. He assesses your decision to have an abortion or to give birth. He knows when you are masturbating. No doubt His sensibilities are offended by your conduct. And if God thing's sensibilities are offended...well... you know how "He" can get. He has a history of smiting entire populations, civilizations and indeed complete species when offended.

Hence the insane behavior and ranting of Fred Phelps, Pat Robertson and their politician minions' adamant demands that women be forced to give birth, that homosexuality be demonized, that the Constitution be amended to prohibit homosexual marriage, etc. To these people, and their constituents, duty is to the God thing first, the country second, individual civil rights last. They are self-appointed agents of their God.

It's not enough for *them* to practice what the "good book" tells them. They have a vested interest in making sure your genitals are applied to the appropriate opposite genitals, your reproductive processes controlled, and that in all things you fit their interpretation of their Bible's definition of morality ... lest God thing get His thong in a twist and vent His wrath on us all.

But my non-Christian, and moderate Christian Republican friends and acquaintances are unmoved by, blind to, this peculiar obsession of their religious Republican brethren; the same brethren who forced Palin's nomination for vice president. They are mostly too old to have abortions, and none are homosexual (or don't admit to being such), and thus could give a fiddler's damn about governmental repression of civil rights by theocratic fanatics. To them it's all about their taxes.

They ignore the potential threat. It's not their issue. Yet the verses of a famous poem keep echoing to me, as it should for all of us:

"...*when they came for the homosexuals I remained silent; I was not a homosexual. And when they came for the Jews I remained silent; I was not a Jew. When they came for me, there was no one left to speak out.*"

73

Let's Keep Christ in Halloween

27 Oct 2008

As Halloween approaches the annual bemoaning of the holy nut jobs starts to rear its empty head. The tradition seems to cause all kinds of consternation with the devout, the same kind that Harry Potter books cause. They fear the festive occasion will provoke allegiance to witchcraft, wizardry, pagan rites and other ungodly heresies. They equate the holiday with devil worship, when in fact the basis of the Celtic pagan religion was reverence of nature, not Satan. Their real fear should be stomachaches and the fat asses kids will get from eating excessive amounts of candy.

Today I saw a poster for a book that's being sold at Barnes & Noble, and Christian book stores. It's entitled *Lets Shine Jesus' Light on Halloween* by Diane Stortz. The cover is a cartoon of a smiling young boy in a costume walking down a neighbor's front path, flash light and goodie bag in hand. Lining the walk are paper bag lanterns with crosses cut into them emitting candle light. This is one of a few Christian books that warn of

Halloween as an insidious attack of unholy influences on their children's devotion to Jesus.

It represents the Christians' need to take what was a pre-Christian pagan Celtic ritual, which was co-opted by the early Catholic Church to be All Saints Day, and what has now evolved purely into a secular day of fun and harmless (usually) activity, and connect it in some whacky way to Jesus, to stick Jesus into where he never belonged. I'm just surprised there hasn't been a movement to dress kids up as the crucified bloodied Jesus and parade them door to door ... *"Treat or Damnation!"* I suppose it's just a matter of time.

But, there's a deeper meaning and positive side to Christians' Halloween hysteria. It is evidence of Christianity's fear of the loss of its base; fear of becoming irrelevant in a modern secular world. That fear is well-founded given the erosion in church attendance, the growth of rationalism and the decline in believers in the modern industrialized world.

While a silly futile overreaction by the dwindling devout, I see it as a positive sign. It's their confirmation and recognition of the decline and eventual death of religiosity. To paraphrase Martha Stewart: *"It's a good thing."*

74

Where are the Atheist Hate Groups?

01 Nov 2008

Question: What do these groups have in common?:

- Fred Phelps' Westboro Baptist Church (homophobic hate group)
- The Christian Identity Movement (anti-Semitic/anti-Black)
- The KKK (anti-Semitic/anti-Black)
- Neo-Nazis/Aryan Nation/Skinheads (anti-Semitic/anti-Black/anti-Gay)
- Phineas Priesthood (anti- race mixing/anti-Semitic)
- Army of God (anti-abortion clinic bombers)
- Institute for Historic Review (anti-Semitic/Holocaust deniers).

Answer: They are all religious-based hate groups. Each claims to endorse "Christian values." Each holds the Bible to be the inerrant "Word of God." Each justifies their hate, violence, discrimination and terror using the scripture. Each recognizes Jesus as their God and savior, albeit, some Nazi groups blend a special form of Aryan paganism with their Christianity.

And these are just a sampling. There are many other groups whose ignorance, hatred and intolerance cause death, destruction, fear, and intimidation under the banner of Christianity.

Liberal and moderate Christians will claim these people are *"not True Christians;"* that they misuse the scripture for their nefarious purposes; that the hate they profess is not supported by the Bible. But it makes no difference. These purveyors of hate love Jesus, and accept him as their savior. Acts do not determine ones Christianity, nor do they affect their salvation; acceptance of Jesus does. That is Christian doctrine. Those hatemongers are as Christian as any of them.

Hate groups aren't limited just to Christians. The Muslims have plenty that cause thousands of deaths, all encouraged by Allah and the Koran. But these Christian hate groups are our own homegrown, flag-waving, God-fearing fellow Americans. Oh, I'd love to say they *"aren't True Americans,"* but by their birth and by our Constitution they are.

I did a Google search for "atheist hate groups". Guess what – there aren't any. Free Thinkers, we Godless heathens, don't band together and picket gay funerals or bomb abortion clinics. We don't create or join groups that burn down African American churches, paint swastikas on synagogues, burn books, or threaten to kill minorities and presidential candidates claiming it to be the will of some unseen entity, endorsed by some ancient scripture. To do those things one seems to need a belief in a god.

Question: Why is that?

75

What Makes a Reverend "Reverend?"

08 Nov 2008

Ever thought about the traditional religious titles of the clergy? "Father," "Your Eminence," and "Reverend" are some of them. Ever wonder how they got those esteemed and elevated titles?

The concept of priest as "Father" goes back to the Catholic Church's insistence that their followers can't relate to or commune directly with their god, but must have an intermediary between the faithful and the deity. That person is in the special position of granting God's forgiveness, giving absolution to their child-like flock; thus, the "father figure." The title comes in particularly handy for priests who like to play a special fatherly role to altar boys and other unsuspecting children. Fathers are to be obeyed, after all. How convenient.

"Eminence" infers a position of superiority, or great achievement, like an eminent surgeon who has made contributions to the profession, and who sets the standard by which all other surgeons are judged. But the Catholic Church endows the title "his Eminence" upon those who have risen through the ranks of delusion and reach the pay grade of Cardinal. The fact that some Cardinals infamously conspired with Nazis, promoted bloodletting during the Inquisition, and participated in persecutions of Jews and "heretics" down through history never seems to result in their losing their title of "superiority." How strange. How telling.

The most common protestant title is "Reverend." The word reverend means *worthy to be revered; entitled to reverence.* But, far from being bestowed only upon those who are truly *"worthy of reverence"* by act or deed, the title is granted to every third-rate charlatan, every under-educated buffoon who ever graduated from a seminary or took a religious correspondence course.

Among the most famous enshrined in the "Illustrious Reverend Hall of Shame" are:

The Rev. Fred Phelps, The Rev. Pat Robertson, The Rev. Jerry Falwell, The Rev. Jesse Jackson, The Rev. Jeremiah Wright, The Rev. Al Sharpton, The Rev. Jim Bakker, The Rev. Jimmy Swaggart, The Rev. Jim Jones, The Rev. John Hagee, The Rev. Ted Haggard, The Rev. Sun Myung Moon, The Rev. Billy Graham, The Rev. D. Spitz, The Rev. Michael Bray. Of course there are thousands of other unnamed men of the cloth who deserve enshrinement. You read about them almost daily, often accompanied by a mug shot.

These vile messengers of hate, fear, and blatant race baiting; opportunists and provocateurs; hypocritical thieves, adulterers, scam artists, murderers, those who suborn murder, domestic terrorists, anti-Semites, pedophiles, and the just plain whack jobs, never seem to lose their *"reverence"* in the eyes of their flock or the media. Somehow their ordination entitles them to be permanently *revered*, regardless of how despicable or egregious their words and deeds.

It's like when you hear a suspected murderer rapist referred to by a police spokesman as *"the Gentleman in question…"* It's a complete non-sequitur, an oxymoron.

So, the next time some guy with a Bible and backward collar tells you he is a "Reverend," don't assume the title to be a guarantee of his integrity, worth, or sanity. And if you shake his hand, count your fingers, wash your hand … rinse, repeat.

76

Christian Proof of God: We'd Better Repent!

12 Nov 2008

Yes... that's right. They have proof of God! Brace yourself, here it is:

"What are the odds that Earth would be placed in orbit the exact distance from the sun to support life? What are the chances that all of the necessary elements to create and support life would conspire to present themselves on Earth? They are infinitesimally small ...Q.E.D. God Did It!! "

Darnn, that's pretty convincing stuff! It seems they have us! But let's broaden our reasoning beyond the cloistered confines of theist thinking.

Certainly if Earth were the only planet in the universe and thus the only platform for life to form, the chances that these things would occur only on this one and only tiny chunk of floating rock would be infinitesimally miniscule. So small that I might even acquiesce, give up my heathen ways, and shout *"Thank ya Jeeezusss!!"*

But what is necessary to remind these Bible-thumping, reality-denying, science-hating folks is this:

> ➢ There are an estimated <u>100 billion galaxies</u> in the universe.

> ➢ Each of those 100 Billion galaxies contains at least <u>10 billion stars</u> (AKA suns).

> ➢ If *conservatively* only ¼ of all those stars have *conservatively* only two planets in their solar system (versus our nine, with Pluto) this equates to approximately <u>250 billion solar systems with 500 billion orbiting planets</u>. This doesn't include solar systems and planets that have become extinct over the past few billion years.

If only one in nine (we are, after all, the only planet of the existing nine in our solar system that is known to support life) of those 500 Billion planets are the necessary distance from their sun to sustain that alien life form, and have the right conditions including an atmosphere, water, organic molecules (or carbon) and other necessary elements, that means the odds are that there are approximately <u>55.6 billion planets</u> out there which are as likely as Earth to provide all of the conditions necessary to form and support life. Don't like that number? Fine, quarter it, make it $1/10^{th}$, $1/100^{th}$, $1/1000^{th}$ of that number. It's still a huge number of potential life-sustaining worlds.

Additionally, a planet's distance from its sun doesn't have to be "exact." There is a "habitable zone," a span of distance from the heat source in which life can flourish. Further still, atmospheric conditions do not have to emulate Earths gaseous composition. Life forms can exist in other than Earth's specific blend of nitrogen, oxygen, argon, and carbon dioxide. It's the limited thinking, the "Earth-centric" mindset of theists that prevents them from incorporating these facts into their half-baked attempted proof of God.

Far from Earth being proof of a sky daddy's unique and singular creation, the "chosen planet" for some deity's divine experiment, it is but one of hundreds of thousands, or millions, or billions of worlds on which life is likely to be reproducing, causing mayhem, destroying their environment, waging war and proffering that THEY are their deity's/deities' chosen planet. The necessary conditions for life to exist on other planets are more likely than not.

Hopefully, those planets have fewer theists than we Earthlings do, and thus are more intelligent, less destructive. But since Earth is the only example we have it doesn't seem promising.

77

Politics, God, and the Future of the Republican Party

16 Nov 2008

The presidential election is over. History has been made. In a few days a new administration, hopefully one less dependent on God's directives, will take power. I'm pretty well up to here with politics for a while. But as the post mortems of the election wind down the big remaining question is *"what's next for the Republican Party?"* It's a critical question. As I see it there are only two paths:

Either the Republican Party will become a reflection of centrist America from a social perspective, and retain its conservative fiscal ideals (which it abandoned over the past eight years); or it will become even more Right socially, more controlled by the religious zealots and more intolerant and exclusionary than it already is.

Either they will take a step back from invoking God as the justification for everything from provoking war in order to spread our brand of democracy at the point of a gun to people who neither want nor respect that objective; or they will continue to embrace it as "God's Plan."

Either they will recognize that marriage between people who love each other irrespective of their sexual orientation neither "picks my pocket nor breaks my leg," as Thomas Jefferson said about people's religious beliefs; or they will continue to try and force their Biblical prohibitions on everyone.

Either they will respect a woman's right to control her reproductive process, and stand aside from impeding medical science's efforts to improve human existence through stem cell research ... even while they themselves may decry it; or they will continue to try and force their beliefs on others and stifle scientific advancement through governmental intervention and obstruction.

Either they will finally accept the separation of church and state as declared in our Constitution, carefully defined by the Founding Fathers' writings, and underscored by the Supreme Court; or they will continue to attempt to make this a "Christian Nation," foist their superstition on others by back door government edict, and continue their attempts to dumb down our schools' science curricula.

The course they choose will determine whether they become a party which embraces the evolution of America's values and thus presents a viable alternative to the Democratic liberal agenda, or if they will surrender the party to the religious nuts, and sink further into a stunted, intolerant, backward mindset that places the prejudices and ignorance of their scripture above 21st century mainstream modernity and secular common sense.

It may take a couple of years to see what faction of the Republican Party emerges victorious. But if the vapid religiosity and stunted intolerance of the Sarah Palin or Mike Huckabee Creationists emerge as leaders; if Republican nominees court the blessings and kiss the rings of the fundamentalist evangelical Right Wing ministry; then it will be clear they have opted to become America's version of the Taliban ... the *"Party of Jesus."*

If that happens, let them rot in their political irrelevance for it.

78

Fossils: A Threat to Faith

21 Nov 2008

The oldest homo sapien remains so far discovered are 195,000 years old. They were unearthed in Ethiopia in 1967. In 2003 the oldest human remains in Europe were discovered and dated as 35,000 years old. In 1958 human remains dating back 13,000 years were found in Colorado, the oldest found in North America thus far.

While all of these findings are accompanied by a +/- factor of a few thousand years the overwhelming evidence is that Man is relatively old. It is corroborated by a variety of testable repeatable methods, and by scientists in a variety of disciplines. It is undeniable.

But it's only undeniable if one accepts reality over blind faith. To more than 40% of Americans, Archbishop James Ussher's 17th century calculation of the Earth as only 6000+ years old based on biblical dating, is pure fact. Ussher declared that God formed the Earth on the night before October 23rd, 4004 BCE, with humans (Adam and Eve) following a few days later.

Some of these folks are just ignorant of scientific discovery. Others, fundamentalists, hard core Evangelicals, know the facts and outright deny them. To them, Ussher's calculation, the Bible's inerrancy, overrule reality, modern science, and corroborating evidence. In the 21st century that's what passes for reason for too many Christians.

Those believers will adamantly insist that radiocarbon dating, sedimentary layering, and every refined measurement at science's disposal are flawed, faulty, inaccurate and thus meaningless. They will present half-truths, pseudo-fact and outright fiction in an attempt to discredit science, as though their faith depends on it. Why? Because their faith depends on it.

To these medieval minded folks, once they admit their book of fables is not a science book, nor a book of history, nor the inerrant word of some super being, then their whole belief system comes into doubt. Their faith will be shaken to its core. Its foundation will collapse. Reality is a threat they will not/cannot tolerate if their belief is to survive. If they were able they would destroy every science book and imprison or burn at the stake every paleontologist, following the example of their early Church predecessors, to halt knowledge, evidence and reason ... the trinity of threat to blind faith.

Instead, they wage a war of myth and misinformation. They build their Creationist museums with dioramas of homo sapiens riding dinosaurs. They home-school their kids, stunting their minds and sacrificing their intellectual growth on the holy altar of blind faith and willful ignorance.

And they will tell their children that someday they can grow up to become candidates for the office of

President of the United States like other famous Creationists: Bush, Huckabee, Brownback, Tancredo and
Palin. And unfortunately, in that regard, they will be
correct.

79

On Thanksgiving Who Does an Atheist Thank?

25 Nov 2008

There are many stories, real and embellished, which speak of the earliest settlers' feasts of thanksgiving in the 17th century. In 1863 Lincoln proclaimed it an annual event *"...as a day of Thanksgiving and Praise to our beneficent Father who dwelleth in the Heavens."* Uh-huh.

So, every fourth Thursday in November believers bow their heads, and presumably mumble some words of groveling thanks to their super being for allowing them to have their turkey, their homes, their jobs, their freedoms, their families, indeed everything that makes America good and life worth living. As an atheist I mumble not.

I have no need of a single day of praise to thank a magical being whose non-influence due to his non-existence has had no effect on anything for which I am grateful. Instead, I have many days of thanksgiving and many people to thank:

- ➤ Every Election Day as I cast my vote, I thank our Founding Fathers for their bravery and foresight.

- ➤ Every Veterans Day and Memorial Day I thank every fallen comrade and every vet who ever fought to acquire and retain our freedoms.

- ➤ Every Columbus Day I am conscious of the contribution of that great explorer.

- ➤ Every Lincolns Birthday and Martin Luther King Day I remember men whose words and deeds set people free.

- ➤ Every Independence Day I reflect on those men and women who risked their lives, fortunes and sacred honor in order to bring this Great Experiment to fruition.

- ➤ Every family birthday, every anniversary and each Thanksgiving Day I am thankful for my family; I thank them for being the people I love and who love me.

Yes, thanks are due, but not to some bogeyman, not to some mythical sky being, not to some imaginary thing that hovers above, or within, or about, or below. Thanks are due to genuine human beings; real men, women, and children past and present whose sacrifices, foresight, commitment, dedication and love made our country unique, and make our lives worthwhile. That's who I'll be thanking on Thanksgiving.

But, if you just can't deal with reality, and must bow and grovel to some unseen god on Thanksgiving Day, may I recommend *Garuda,* the Hindu bird god. He's as close to a turkey god as you can get.

80

Satiating God's Blood Lust, Again

01 Dec 2008

Dateline: Mumbai, India
A Muslim terrorist cell creates havoc throughout the city.
Hostages taken. Blood of the innocent flows in the streets.

Ah, how those theists love to appease their God with blood letting. What's the latest bodycount from India where Muslims, were killing Hindus, Jews, and Christians with delightful abandon? 175?

To those who would try to downplay the religious factor, and call this attack politically inspired, please... spare us. Muslims comprised 100% of the perpetrators. And given that eight or nine Jews were executed among an Indian Jewish population of something on the order of approximately 0.00001% of the population pretty much eliminates their deaths being attributed to chance.

Was the hate for the infidel, and the enthusiastic murderous acts of those Muslim terrorists fed by Allah's or Mohammed's promise of a paradise complete with the reward of eternal virgins? Count on it.

Among the families of the deceased Jews, is their loss made more bearable by the martyrdom of their loved ones? Perhaps.

Does the belief of Christians that their beloved family members now reside with Jesus salve the pain and diminish the anguish of the senselessness of their loved ones deaths? Surely.

Is the suffering of the surviving families of the Hindu victims relieved by knowing that their dead will be reincarnated? Probably.

Did the believing victims pray for mercy and beg for their lives in their last moments of terror? No doubt. Did their beliefs calm their horror, make it all okay? You tell me. We know for certain, it didn't save their lives.

Now, imagine there were no delusions of supernaturalism, no promise of paradise or any life after death. Imagine no adamant claims of "the only TRUE way" fanning hatred and intolerance of beliefs that are equally moronic to one's own. Imagine if all people were free of the religious slave mentality. Imagine no need for platitudes, justifications and myths. Imagine those 175 people still alive. Imagine no religion.

81

What Would it Take for You to Believe in....

06 Dec 2008

What would it take to convince you alien abductions, Bigfoot, UFO spacecraft, ghosts, witches, ESP, the Loch Ness Monster, demons, haunted houses, etc., are real?

For me, and I'd like to believe for a majority of people, it would take irrefutable proof, a preponderance of scientifically supported and testable evidence. And yet many people actually accept these things as real based on hearsay, a hack author's convincing fiction, the flimsiest of questionable evidence.

For these people it's unimportant that none of those mythical beings have ever been irrefutably identified, or the pseudo-scientific or supernatural phenomena ever held up to a single controlled experiment. To the confirmed believer it's enough to just "want to believe", lack of genuine evidence doesn't matter.

Imagine a child who was born to parents who were avid UFO believers; who accompanied their folks to UFO conventions from an early age; who read their parents' UFO books and magazines, of which there are thousands; who year after year overhear their parents and their parents' friends talking about the latest sightings and the government's efforts to cover it up. What are the odds that such a child would become a dyed in the wool UFO devotee, and consider anyone who didn't believe in UFOs deniers of "Truth," or "deceived fools?" I'd guess near 100%.

Now, substitute for UFO believer parents, parent believers in God/Jesus and all the superstitious baggage that comes with it and you'd have the exact same impact on the impressionable child. The conditions that breed one unscientific, unproven, irrational belief are the same for all of them.

And just as any committed UFO advocate will dismiss other popular mythical delusions as crazy and absurd, so theists dismiss all other religions/gods as delusions or false beliefs. Coincidence? Hardly.

Even as they read this the connection will be dismissed by theists as unrelated to THEIR particular belief. Their minds can't allow them to even acknowledge it. It's a blind spot in their psyche.

82

Gods I Can Accept

11 Dec 2008

*"Well, if you don't believe in God, you must think
YOU'RE God."*
"If you don't worship God, what DO you worship?"

Likely if you've ever been in more than a passing
conversation with a fundie you've been on the receiving end of similar statements and questions.
It's thrown down like a gauntlet, a challenge.

The problem this exposes is theist inability to conceive of anyone not having belief in the supernatural.
They can't fathom anyone not being dependent on
some "greater power" than themselves; are incapable
of believing people can lead perfectly happy and normal lives without being a slave to the religious meme,
and kowtowing to some ancient myth.

So in the future, instead of trying to explain how
rejection of all god concepts from Zeus to Isis to Jesus,
et al requires no substitute, I'm going to declare my
"gods." I'll tell them that my gods are Reason, Reality, Logic, and the Never Ending Quest for Knowledge

through Discovery. Their power is manifested in the "trinity" of Rationalism, Empiricism and Naturalism. Its "church/temple/mosque/synagogue" resides within my mind.

I'll say I worship Critical Thinking; the Scientific Method; Supportable Evidence; Man's Drive, Desire and Ability to Learn; his desire to break free from the darkness of superstition and the blind belief born of nomadic Bronze Age sand people, or 2nd century cultists, or Hellenistic seers, or aboriginal shamans.

My gods demand no tithing, no praying, no kneeling, no sacrifice, no vestments, no sacred undergarments, no hymns, no holidays in their honor. No symbolic consumption of human flesh or blood is necessary. It neither threatens eternal damnation, nor dangles a promise of eternal reward. It doesn't demand blind belief with no evidence of the nonexistent or the lockstep acceptance of any of its theories.

My gods' only doctrine is continued expansion of knowledge; revising understanding as new discoveries warrant; not fearing to admit we don't know what we don't yet know; exchanging ideas grounded in reality; weighing hard evidence, being discerning, and making informed decisions unencumbered by any predetermined or mandated agenda. That we allow ourselves to recognize how much we've learned, how far we've come, and how much more we can learn when not shackled to the ancient fears and ignorance of supernaturalism and religious dogma.

My gods have only two commandments:

1. "Ask questions and seek answers grounded in reality."

2. "Education is a sacrament. Read, Live, Learn"

83

Ice Storms, New Hampshire, and Acts of God

13 Dec 2008

Thirty minutes ago our electricity was restored after the worst ice storm in New Hampshire history knocked out power for half of the residents of the state. My power was out for almost forty hours. There remain upwards of 300,000 NH families still without it. They say power may not be fully restored for many more days, perhaps a week or more in some areas.

It wasn't so bad for Mrs. Hump, the dogs and I. We have an automatic propane generator that came on at 3 a.m. Friday and gave us all the normal comforts we enjoy.

By midafternoon Friday, all of our neighbors without generators had been called and invited to come over, take hot showers, fill water jugs and buckets for drinking and flushing (wells don't pump without electricity), and generally enjoy the warmth of our wood burning stove, hot soup and ample beer and liquor supply. Fortunately everyone around here has an alternate heat source, woodstoves and fireplaces, so there were no life threatening situations in spite of temperatures dipping into single digits overnight.

The Governor declared a state of emergency and the National Guard was deployed to help clear downed trees from streets. Old folks with no alternate heat source were evacuated to community shelters or neighbors spare rooms. FEMA provided emergency facilities with generators and cots; the Red Cross went into action. Thus far there has only been one death attributed to the storm. As natural disasters go, this one was well handled.

As I reflected on the myriad stories carried by our two local papers and the TV news coverage which preempted all regular TV programming for days, I realized I never once heard the words *"Act of God"* or *"Miracle."* or *"By God's Grace"* uttered by a single reporter, nor any of the scores of storm victims interviewed. Not a single, *"Thank you, Jesus!"* Not one reference to God's *"merciful divine intervention,"* or the angry pronouncement of *"His divine punishment for New Hampshire's sinful, ungodly, or ... uh... err ... maple syrupy ways!"*

Had a similar natural occurrence happened in some other states (read: Bible Belt), every televangelist, all of the two-bit Bible-banging clergy and their frenzied faithful, would be wailing in the streets and getting face time on every camera testifying, attributing their lot, lives and narrow escapes to the supernatural; explaining the mystical cause or meaning of the event; declaring its impact on their state as the *"Lord's Will!"* perhaps even a sign of His displeasure.

But nope, not in New Hampshire. Not a single supernatural platitude was to be found.

New Englanders are famously self-sufficient and pragmatic. We understand natural occurrences, weather changes; we attribute to them no supernatural cause or purpose. We are an educated people and don't tolerate fools lightly. We include the overtly religious under that latter classification.

Our lack of gullibility makes New Hampshire a not-so-fertile field for proselytizing, thus keeping the numbers of religious fanatics in the state to the bare minimum. The few that remain are largely mute. It's not unlike how the cold climate helps keep us free of termites. I love New Hampshire.

84

Why Oil and Fundamentalist Christianity Don't Mix

18 Dec 2008

With all the focus on fossil fuels and the price of gasoline, it leads me to wonder how exactly do "Young Earth" fundie Christians explain the formation of crude oil?

Virtually every accredited geologist on Earth agrees that crude oil was formed by the decomposition of organic materials, plants and animals, in an airless environment of 60 to 120 degrees Celsius, under enormous pressure, for between 10 and 300 million years. There are reams of scientific evidence for this process. There is another not widely held hypothesis called abiogenic petroleum origin, which doesn't require organic materials to form petroleum, but even that is predicated on an Earth that is billions of years old.

So what do the Young Earthers say? *The Great Flood did it!!* It buried trees and animals under sediment (in 40 days). The speed at which this occurred created enormous pressure and heat, which created oil.

Unfortunately, this simplistic and short cycle oil "creationism" can't be supported by laboratory testing, scientific principles, or layered fossil evidence, nor can they offer any substantiation that demonstrates its efficacy in any scientifically sound way.

What Young Earthers offer is religious babble, because Creationist ideas do not have to be scientifically sound or supportable; they need only be sound within the realm of creationist dogma; ergo *"God made the Earth* <u>appear</u> *as if it was 100's of millions of years old."* Well, that's that! When someone invokes intentional deception by a Supreme Being or magic as the answer to anything, it pretty much puts the kibosh on any reasonable discourse. They are worshiping a God that needs to test his creations' faith by making Earth look older than it really is. As Coral Yoshi said, *"That's a God with some serious self esteem issues."*

You won't find any Creationists with petro-geology degrees working for oil companies; but more than one is employed by the Creation Museum, and probably KFC.

85

Christmas Approaches, Let's Honor the True Meaning of the Season

21 Dec 2008

On December 25th, 4 CE, a child was said to have been born to a Jewish virgin as she and her husband traveled to the place of his birth to be taxed by the Romans. A bright star shone over the birthplace so that the faithful would know. And so began the Good News of the birthday of the Messiah, the Son of Man, and God's Only Son.

Of course, there is neither written record of, nor any precedence for, the uprooting of entire populations and requiring them to relocate to places they don't reside in order to collect taxes. Neither was any special star evident. Nor do pregnant virgins exist – either then or now. In fact, there are no corroborating eyewitness accounts of any such star, taxation exodus, or personage of Jesus outside of the Bible.

We do know that December 25th was an important day to the Romans. On that day each year was held the festival of Dies Natalis Solis Invicti, *"the birthday of the unconquered sun.*" It marked the pagan celebration of the winter solstice, when the shortest day of the year which occurs between the 20th and 23rd each year, reverses, signaling the lengthening of days. To many pagan cultures the Sun WAS god and life giver. Indeed, if anything could justify worship it would be the life-giving sustenance of the Sun. The cult of the Christians simply co-opted the pagan observance, substituting the rites of "rebirth of the Sun" with the "birth of The Son" just as they co-opted so many other pagan myths, holidays and practices for their hybrid blend of Pagan/Abrahamic belief systems.

But none of that is important. What is important is that this man-god worshipping death cult which marks its deity's birth on December 25th, has persevered for almost 2000 years. With it came almost as many years of deception, misery, intolerance, hatred, persecution, torture, subjugation, intimidation, ignorance and murder by its devoted followers in the name of their God.

So as you open presents under the pagan tree, huddle around the burning pagan Yule log, and celebrate the lengthening of the days, take a moment to remember the true meaning and reason for the Season. Feel free to offer a toast of happy birthday to Sun gods Sol Invictus, Ra, Helios and Apollo. Be sure to thank them for the warming rays of their countenances, and for not having inspired their followers to self righteous persecution in their name. Merry Winter Solstice

86

Proof of God's Non-Existence: Let a Jury Decide

27 Dec 2008

While the burden of proof for God's existence is on believers, since they are making a positive assertion, I've often thought about what would constitute proof that no Supreme Being(s) exist.

In a court of law, when hard evidence is not available (i.e. deposable eyewitnesses, fingerprints, forensics, DNA, et al) lawyers depend on circumstantial evidence. Circumstantial evidence is acceptable and often compelling. The prevailing accepted criterion to convince a jury in a civil case is by a "preponderance of evidence," circumstantial or otherwise.

I propose that there is a preponderance of circumstantial evidence to show God(s) does not/do not exist.

1. Dispelled Supernatural Explanations- the Diminished God:

The scientific age is in its infancy. It is said that more discoveries have been made in the past 300 years than have taken place in the past 5,000 years. The infallibility of the Catholic Church has been all but dispelled as they capitulate to Copernicus' model, and placidly accept Darwinian Theory, albeit, blending it with their God's "divine plan". What for millennia the faithful attributed to the supernatural such as the "wrath of God" (i.e. earthquakes, lightning strikes, drought, extreme weather, plague); the "work of Satan" (i.e. deformed births, two-headed sheep, plague); "demonic possession/witches" (i.e. epilepsy, hysteria, catatonic states); all have been shown by man's scientific awakening to be natural, explainable, even reproducible/repeatable events, and processes.

Similarly, radiocarbon dating, consistency of fossil species evidence within geologic strata, and other measurements both terrestrial and cosmologic which meet stringent scientific criteria, provide overwhelming evidence of an Old Earth and the efficacy of Evolutionary Theory; rendering Creationism and Young Earth fables just that ... unsupportable fables with no scientific basis.

Thus, while the gaps in our knowledge still exist, they are steadily shrinking. Along with the shrinking gaps the "God of the Gaps" has diminished and continues to do so exponentially. I submit therefore, that each and every theist, clergy or layman, living or dead, who has ever acquiesced to the scientific explanation of what was once a pre-scientific, biblically endorsed, theistically held belief (i.e. earth as center of the universe; a firmament; plague as punishment, etc.), is himself a witness to and proof that what theists once attributed to God's Word or power is fallacy. Thus, this God's credibility has diminished as "God did it!" explanations were dispelled by those discoveries.

If a god was all powerful, all knowing in his attributes, the power he held over what we now recognize as natural events could not be diminished commensurate with his lowly creations' discoveries and intellectual growth. Q.E.D. God does not exist.

2. No Probable Cause for Belief:

The Bible is the sole document in support of the God of Abraham and supernatural Jesus. In 3,500+ years since the Old Testament, and 1,800 years since the New Testament, no new evidence has ever been produced proving supernatural events described therein actually occurred. No corroborating eyewitness statements by disinterested parties exist, any archaeological evidence, any scientific proofs or discoveries that substantiate the source documents.

For almost two millennia there have been numerous documented predictions by theists of the "end of times"/"second coming". None of these predictions have come true.

Similarly, no new "miracles" have been forthcoming that could not be explained in natural terms. The "age of miracles," it seems, has inexplicably disappeared with the advent of growth in knowledge of the natural world, and the scientific age.

If a Supreme Being existed who genuinely cared about its creations believing in him, common logic infers he would reveal his existence in undeniable and proof positive terms. He would do so without the need for fallible human interpretation, or suppression/suspension of the human ability to reason and logic (which presumably this God bestowed upon them). Retention of faith would not be dependent on man-made excuses and apologetics for the absence of this God's personal appearance.

3. Statistical Probability – Historical Falsification and Rejection:

Throughout Man's history, gods have been part of every civilization and culture. There were thousands of god's worshiped by thousands of religions, cults and sects, many of them still practiced in remote areas of the globe. There has never been a shred of objective evidence to suggest any of these thousands of mythical beings were genuine. Thus, every theist alive today rejects those defunct gods as simply the product of Man's imagination, delusion, or in extreme cases "the deception of Satan." Every believer today is convinced that only <u>THEIR</u> God(s) are genuine, even while they have no more evidence of their Gods' existence than did the ancient pagan practitioners.

Since none of the old gods are accepted as real by current day believers, and since all of the current competing gods are held to be true only by their respective devotees, statistically and logically there exists no reason to accept that ANY concept of a supernatural being is genuine. It simply defies the lessons of history and probability.

In summary: The evidence for the supernatural or God should be held to no higher or lower standard than the evidence for any other unobservable mythical being. I submit that in the absence of said evidence there is no probable cause to believe in the existence of any God/gods.

Virtually all theists have on their side is "hearsay," which is the least valued of all evidence. So what can we deduce? This: If logic, reason and a preponderance of evidence were the sole basis for a ruling, these arguments alone would stand as overwhelming evidence for proof of no God.

Of course, my premise is based on a court of law scenario, where the judge and jury are impartial, bound by the rule of law to decide by a preponderance of evidence irrespective of the personal opinion of the participants, or their own beliefs. Unfortunately, given the lack of intellect of jurors, and their inability to overcome their own mental enslavement to religion, I doubt an impartial jury could be found. Certainly not in the Bible Belt, or among justices Roberts, Scalia, Alito, or Thomas.

87

Happy New Year...the World is Going to End!!

01 Jan 2009

If you're reading this, you survived New Years Eve. Happy 2009! That's the good news. The bad news is this means you have about three years and eleven months to prepare yourself for the End of the World.

Yes, prepare to bend over and kiss your arse goodbye because the Mayan calendar runs out December 21, 2012. If you buy into the hype, the world will likewise run out on that date. And, if you believe everything you read on the internet, Nostradamus wrote a quatrain that confirms the same year and the Hopi Indians concur. Hey, what more proof does one need?

Christians have always loved end of world predictions. They've been predicting it since the New Testament. They have a word, eschatology, which means the study of the end of the world in religious terms. There have been literally thousands of end time predictions down through the ages. Usually it's Christians making them – always they are wrong, obviously.

Invariably the prophet of doom attributes the failed prediction to a mathematical miscalculation. Often they will recalculate a new date. That one turns out wrong as well. Interestingly, the devotees of the cult's religious leader often retain their belief and maintain their faith even when the date comes and goes, and they are left standing befuddled on a hill top without having beamed up. The Jehovah's Witnesses are famous for this, but it's not exclusively their idiocy.

Evangelicals, Born Agains, expect the End Times to occur in their lifetime they just don't like setting dates. They've learned from experience not to be too specific… it's just too embarrassing. However, to the theistically infirm death-desiring crowd, every hurricane, earthquake, forest fire, draught, tidal wave, war, dip in the stock market, rise in oil prices, or the election of an African-American president, is a harbinger of the coming Rapture.

But this 2012 thing has taken on a whole new dimension. Along with the usual Christian sheep who are prone to believing anything, every buffoon who believes in alien visitations, 9/11 conspiracy, psychokinetic energy, mind reading government satellites, astrology, etc., has contracted End of World Fever.

With the economic downturn we're in, I'm trying to figure out how to cash in on this hysteria to supplement my income. End Time T-shirts? Holy crash helmets? Rapture insurance? Mayan calendars with nude camel pinups?

Given the intellectual capacity of believers this could be a gold mine!

88

Got Spirituality?

05 Jan 2009

"I'm not religious, but I'm spiritual."

If I had a nickel for every time I've heard someone say that I'd have … well, $1.35. Frankly, I have no clue as to what they are talking about. The term "spiritual" comes with very heavy religious connotations; words like "supernatural," "soul," "incorporeal," "sacred" and "ecclesiastical" pepper its definitions.

I view theist "spirituality" as part of their dogmatic mumbo jumbo. My position on them is pretty well established. Similarly, I dismiss nonreligious/non-theists who call themselves "spiritual" as quasi-super naturalists worthy of suspicion if not outright contempt.

The closest as I can come to understanding "spirituality" as a concept to which I can relate is looking at the sky on a clear night, or an alpine view on a clear day, or the Sequoia National Forest on a misty autumn morning, or hearing Beethoven's 9th, and being moved to say "Wow!" in response to the awe and grandeur it evokes in me.

It's human appreciation for the majestic beauty of the planet without breaking it down into its natural/material elements. It speaks to our innate wonderment for the complexity and vastness of the universe, the reality of our utter insignificance/unimportance to it; or admiration for the beauty of man's creativity, technology, great literary works, or symphonies; or reverence and respect for a well-structured scientific theory or philosophical concept.

To be emotionally invested in, or moved by, those natural phenomena is peculiar to humans. It's entirely natural, nothing spiritual about it. I imagine that one who cannot experience that kind of awe or emotion is devoid of imagination, and is empathetically and/or intellectually defunct, possibly even sociopathic.

On the other hand, those touting their holy, esoteric, mystical, magical spiritualism are either sanctimonious gullible theists or New Age sheeple. Both are to be avoided or ridiculed mercilessly.

89

Atheist Axioms

10 Jan 2009

Educated people understand that atheism has no dogma, doctrine or dictates. The only qualification to be an atheist is to hold no belief in a God or gods.

However, there is certain commonality of ideas, precepts and axioms – whatever one wants to call them – that seem to be shared by most Freethinkers. Whether one had these ideas, and thus became atheist as a result, or developed these ideas as a result of their becoming atheist is unclear to me. Possibly it's both. I tend toward the former.

The following is a list of those ideas/axioms. They are not entirely my own; I have added to the list, revised and expanded upon them. They come from *The Secular Web* at Infidels.com. It's a great resource website for atheists, or those wishing to understand atheism. Here's their link: http://www.infidels.org/library/modern/mathew/intro.html

Here are those axioms for your consideration:

- Morality is not predetermined; it evolves and is defined by a culture/civilization to describe how that culture ought to work for the betterment of the group.
- Be especially skeptical of extraordinary positive assertions. Extraordinary assertions require extraordinary evidence before they can be embraced.
- If you want your life to have some sort of "meaning" beyond procreation and continuation of the species, it's up to you, the individual, to develop that meaning.
- There are no absolutes.
- Search for what is true, even if it makes you uncomfortable or the answer is counter to your preexisting hypothesis.
- Relying on some external power to change you is self deception; you must change yourself. Every person is responsible/accountable for their lives and actions.
- Just because something is popular, widely believed, or has been believed for a long time, doesn't mean it's true or good.
- Don't accept anything as real simply because you want it to be true.
- All beliefs or hypotheses are open to challenge, questioning, and should be subjected to testing by the scientific method when possible.
- Make the most of your life, it's the only one you'll have.

This isn't a test. There is no pass or fail. These aren't laws. Agreement or objection to any of these axioms doesn't determine your atheism, or disqualify you as a non-believer. Only theists do that kind of thing. Theses are simply offered as a list of precepts founded in reality, and are generally accepted by modern Freethinking people (and ancient Freethinkers as well). It's an informal declaration of freedom from the encumbrances of managed thinking mandated by theistic belief for thousands of years.

Note that none of them recommend dietary laws, insist that you kill your disobedient child, or establish how to treat your slaves, etc. You're on your own with that stuff.

90

Water Boarding, Hypocrisy &
Theism: A Holy Trinity

15 Jan 2009

I was listening to the confirmation hearing of Attorney General Nominee Eric Holder on NPR today. I have a few bones to pick with him related to his Bill Clinton days and his ultra liberal views, but all in all he's qualified for the job and will be confirmed.

But the big headline that came out of today's hearing is that Holder stated that water boarding is torture, as though that is some kind of revelation. Anyone who knows how water boarding is conducted, what it does, would recognize it as torture. The US prosecuted Japanese military officers for using the technique on American POWs in WWII. They were hung as war criminals. Water boarding was inflicted on heretics during the Inquisition to get them to see the error of their ways.

So who claims water boarding is not torture? What kind of disingenuous, completely ignorant, or self-deceiving hypocrite would believe it NOT to be torture? George W. Bush, self-proclaimed Born Again Christian; Dick Cheney, Methodist; Donald Rumsfeld, disgraced

Secretary Of Defense under Bush, Presbyterian; John Ashcroft, disgraced Attorney General under Bush, Assembly of God - Born Again Christian; Alberto Gonzalez, disgraced Attorney General under Bush, Catholic.

The list is endless! Just about every Right Wing, Evangelical, Jesus-loving, God-fearing Christian in Congress, on a Conservative radio talk show, or behind the televangelist pulpit, denies water boarding is torture. Yet, I do not know of a single atheist familiar with the technique who denies water boarding is torture.

How can this be? The evidence is overwhelming; the precedence of WWII prosecutions of Japanese officers for using the method is glaring; the fact that it is inflicted only on those from whom we wish to extract information is telling. If anyone has any doubt and wanted empirical evidence one way or another, all they'd have to do is submit themselves to water boarding and within a minute or two they'd have a firsthand evidence.

What it all leads to are these conclusions:

- Evidence and fact mean nothing to fanatical theists. Once they "believe" something, evidence and facts are inconveniences to be ignored and denied.
- Christians seem to have a proclivity for torture. Perhaps a trait stemming from the Inquisitions and witch trials. A God-given right, it would seem.
- Fanatical Christians are hypocrites, recognizing torture only when Christians are the victims. It's never torture when <u>they</u> administer it, when it suits their agenda.
- Christian torture deniers shun the scientific method, and thus would never voluntarily submit themselves to the test … believing a fallacy is enough.
- The much vaunted higher ethics and morality of Christians is a bald faced lie.

91

Being Intolerant of Intolerance: Where's the Dilemma?

27 Jan 2009

Recently I posited that it wouldn't bother me a whole lot if Rick Warren, Evangelical minister, homophobe activist, etc., died an early, natural death. Frankly, there is enough intolerance and oppression that those who promulgate it, who are its poster boys, have no value to me or a freedom-loving society, as far as I am concerned.

Voicing this in an atheist blog I was chastised by a fellow nonbeliever:

"Who is allowed to set the standard on what "tolerance" is? A follower of Warren's can easily point out that you're being intolerant of Warren and his views."

Well, to paraphrase Supreme Court Justice Brennan's famous quote about pornography: *"I may not be able to adequately define intolerance, but I know it when I see it."* There is a vast difference between someone being intolerant of granting full human rights to a minority, and describing my disgust for Warren and my wish for his natural demise as intolerant. The difference is plain: My wish to see Warren suffer a natural early death does not stand in the way of his First Amendment rights to preach, endorse, or practice his intolerance. My ill wishes toward him do nothing to impede his rights, have no measurable effect.

On the other hand, Warren's supernatural doctrine, which drives his speech, activism, actions, and that of his followers, directly obstructs attainment of equal rights for those whose lifestyle and sex practices are different from his/their own. Attainment of those rights would not encroach on Warren's rights to practice his lifestyle, sexual behavior, or beliefs. His actions have had a measurable effect on people's liberties, most recently in California on Proposition 8. That's intolerance.

If my disgust for Warren and wish for his demise is intolerant then we may as well call abolitionists "intolerant" for their vocal opposition to slavery and slave owners. Would anyone have called anti-Nazi sentiment "intolerant", and thus comparable to the intolerant anti-Semitic genocidal actions of the Nazis themselves? Such a concept would be a perversion of the term "intolerant."

At best I can be described as radically opposed to prejudice and injustice and thus "intolerant of intolerance." At worst I can be tagged as a mean-spirited-death-wishing-godless-heathen. Albeit, to a Nazi, a slave owner, or a Christian homophobe activist, calling my attitude and ill wishes toward them "intolerant" might make sense ... but only to them, and thus who gives a damn?

92

Abortion: A Theist Speaks for God

01 Feb 2009

While religious fanatics are rare in New Hampshire, we do have a few scattered about. The following letter to the editor appeared in my local newspaper:

"I am coming to the conclusion that God made every baby for a purpose. God had a plan for us before we were even formed, so He does have a plan for every baby. He loves all of us, including the unborn. People are made in God's image, they are humans. We need to respect our fellow humans."

– Jon, Winchester, NH

What Jon doesn't get here is that his brief and no doubt heartfelt letter is just chock-full of fallacies, delusion and contradiction. Let's dissect it:

"I am coming to the conclusion that God made every baby for a purpose."

Jon didn't come to any such conclusion. The conclusion was provided to him as an interpretation of theist doctrine that has likely been fed to him since childhood; the very same doctrine that concluded for him that there was a God in the first place. For Jon to suggest he came to the conclusion as a result of independent thought and analysis is self deception, or intellectual dishonesty.

"God had a plan for us before we were even formed, so He does have a plan for every baby." Really? So the spontaneous abortions, miscarriages, stillbirths, all natural events which represent approximately 50% of fetal deaths in the US were part of God's plan for those babies? They were planned by the Supreme Abortionist as what … land fill? Nice plan.

And what, exactly, was God's plan for the zygotes that became Hitler, Jim Jones, David Koresh, Timothy McVeigh, the 9/11 terrorists, etc.? His plan was for them was to be born to destroy, cause suffering, pain, death and horror? They were born as part of God's plan to help thin the population of European Jews, gullible Christian believers, millions of innocent Cambodians and the populations of Oklahoma City and New York City?

Since God knows in advance the outcome of all things, God's plans thus must be psychopathically inspired. You'd think a sane and omniscient God would have planned better by causing those fiend babies to be spontaneously aborted. I guess not.

"He loves all of us, including the unborn."

Well, God sure has a strange way of showing his love. I love my sons, but I don't demonstrate that love by subjecting them to hideous and agonizingly painful deaths by AIDS, Ebola, starvation, dysentery, etc. as this God seems to do to his children. They die this way by the tens of thousands each day throughout the third world... infants, toddlers.

These children had no "free will" to choose either their lot in life, or their religion; a merciful all-knowing and loving God would recognize that, one would think. God, it seems, just loves those kids to death.

"People are made in God's image, they are humans."

Christian apologists will tell us that the Bible means "character" when it says "image." They claim image does not mean "physical form." But more to the point, Jon's sentiment suggests God is human. Actually, Man created God in Man's image. All gods have the same jealousy, anger, vindictiveness and remarkable capacity for inhuman treatment toward their "creations" as man has toward his fellow man ...only more so. The Old Testament testifies to that. All subsequent New Testament divine personality changes and makeovers are the result of Man's doing as well.

Naturally all this would be dismissed by Jon in the usual manner of the theist apologists: *"God works in strange and mysterious ways."; "Who are we to understand God's plan?"; "God's mercy in killing those children IS his love."* etc., etc., etc. ... ad infinitum.

As a spokesman for his deity, Jon falls flat. The only thing Jon got right in his letter was his admonishment to respect our fellow human beings. One needn't invoke a god, or imbue a bundle of embryonic cells with humanity to do that. Jon got one out of five sentences correct, 20% out of a possible 100%. In theist think, that's a passing mark.

93

The Bible, True Science and the Historical Resurrection

07 Feb 2009

"I'm a Christian. The most important event in history is the resurrection of Jesus of Nazareth. I believe true science does not contradict the Bible."

So reads the personal profile of a 58-year-old internet message group member. He actually believes the Bible to be a history book and science book.

I could understand that coming from a monk or peasant in the Dark Ages, but there's been way too much water under the bridge of understanding and discovery for any adult with a functioning brain stem to make such absolute and unyielding statements in the 21st century.

Let's take his belief that the myth of Jesus' resurrection is "history" (it's as much history as is the Mormon belief that the Angel Moroni gave Joseph Smith gold tablets to translate). He is saying it supersedes in importance the following historical events:

*Man's migration out of Africa and the subsequent popula-
tion of the world;*
Man's mastery of fire and the invention of the wheel;
*The Neolithic Age where man established agrarian societ-
ies, leaving nomadic existence and settling into communi-
ties, and laying the foundation for human culture;*
*The development of the first written laws for human be-
havior, i.e. the Hebrew Ten Commandments, The Code of
Hammurabi, etc.;*
*The advent of Greek philosophy, mathematics, govern-
ment and social structure which were the foundation for
our modern Western civilization.*

Had none of these, or indeed only <u>one</u> of these genuine historical events not taken place the world as we know it today would not exist. But the mythical rising of a mythical dead man-god who is rejected by two-thirds of the world as either myth or not pivotal in their existence, <u>that</u> is what passes as the most important historical event according to this theistically handicapped unfortunate. Hell, the discovery of germs, micro-organisms, and the invention of modern sanitation has more historical value than a mythical zombie's resuscitation as far as I'm concerned.

Then there's the *"true science doesn't contradict the Bible"* claim. The sciences of physics, biology, astronomy, geology, all the hard disciplines, contradict and reject:

*The concept of a domed firmament over the planet with
stars set into it;*
People living to eight hundred years old;
The Creation story;
*The ability to see the entire Earth from a mountain top
(i.e. a flat Earth);*

The ability for life on Earth to survive a cessation of rotation of the planet (the sun stopping in the sky; Joshua 10:13);

The ability to reanimate and restore to life three day old dead corpses;

The ability for two each of millions of species to fit on a boat;

Therefore, by this Christian's definition, it renders those scientific disciplines, *"not true science[s]."*

This theist's lack of reasoning goes beyond denial. It is self-imposed ignorance, rejection of prima fascia evidence, a complete regression into Dark Age thinking. I wonder if he suffers witches to live.

94

Prayers for a Child Killer

18 Feb 2009

Casey Anthony killed her 2-year-old toddler Caylee in Florida last year. There is a preponderance of circumstantial evidence, totaling five-hundred pages. She hid the child's body. It was months before the remains were found near the grandparents' house. The case has been dragging on for eight months. Anthony has been stonewalling police efforts to get information to nail the case shut evading questions about her failure to report the child missing for a month, lying to investigators multiple times, etc.

Last week a news report appeared that a pastor is organizing a prayer vigil for accused child murderer Casey Anthony to give her *"hope and comfort."* In discussing the absurdity of this misplaced Christian goodness, one of the faithful offered this:

"There's no harm done here, if you don't believe prayer does anything then that's it, it just doesn't.... but these people do, and at least they're putting forth the effort to give hope in

the way they think is right to do so. They're just doing the best, the best way they know how to. That's true love."

My reply follows:

Thank you for that genuine Christian gibberish.

That praying for a child murderer, or anyone, has no effect isn't at all the issue. *"Effort to give hope ...?"* Hope for what? Hope for a hung jury; a verdict of not guilty; of escaping the death penalty or life in prison? Hope for another child for her to raise and kill; hope she'll go to heaven in spite of her heinous deed? And why, for a mother who murders her child and feels no remorse nor takes responsibility?

The problem with the mindlessly devout is that they cannot discern between people who are worthy of sympathy, whose misfortunes evoke empathy, and those who are due only societies disgust, revulsion, condemnation and punishment.

But I am unsurprised. Christian doctrine tells murderers, rapists, genocidal maniacs, et al, they will get their reward in a celestial candy land as long as they telepathically promise some alleged dead man-god that he is their master, then symbolically eat his body and drink his blood. Then all is forgiven. All the while the same doctrine claims innocents like Anne Frank and humanitarian scientists like Jonas Salk burn in hell. Frankly, it's a despicable and obscene doctrine; one that would likely disgust Jesus himself.

The absence of Ms. Anthony's humility, civility, humanity, accountability for her actions, since they mean nothing to Christian salvation doctrine, is easily overlooked and not highly valued by the faithful. That she is offered sympathy and support for murdering her child makes me want to retch. More so does the sanctimonious justification for such inane acts of symbolic Christian benevolence.

One has to wonder if it's because she is a self-proclaimed Christian that she is the recipient of the flock's good wishes. Do Christians make distinctions among Christian, pagan, atheist, Jewish and Muslim child murderers? If so why? Will the devout hold a prayer vigil for Bin Laden when he is captured and faces legal judgment? Is he not equally entitled to, worthy of, their love, their comfort and their hopeful prayers? Or perhaps it's only the Christian murderers of innocent children and not Muslim murderers of 3,000 adult Americans who warrant these good Christians' love and platitudes.

I can't determine which disgusts me more: The grotesqueness of the doctrine, the idiocy of the gesture, or the Christian hypocrisy.

95

God of the Ants

22 Feb 2009

When I was a child I had an ant farm, one of those plastic frames with clear sides filled with sand. You could watch the ants digging and doing their ant thing. I diligently fed them sugar and water. I watched them build their tunnels, never interfering with their daily goings on. They had the ant version of Free Will and manna from heaven.

Had these ants possessed reasoning ability, they would have probably worshipped me as their source of life, their god. Certainly my benevolence and omnipotence would be evident. I was the life giver.

What these ants were totally unaware of is that this same god that gave them sustenance was also a wrathful god. I used to bait wild ant hills with sugar, wait for the colony to swarm, then encircle and crisscross the mass of wild ants with highly flammable model airplane glue and set it on fire. There was no escape. There were never any survivors. It was utter ant genocide. Not even the virgin female ant was taken captive.

Clearly if these ants could think it would have been perceived as the act of an angry vengeful god wreaking divine punishment for some inexplicable ant sin.

Eventually I became bored with the ant farm. They were flushed down the toilet, or dispersed into exile in the wilderness, I can't recall which. It was the ant version of the Diaspora, The Great Flood, or maybe the Rapture.

So, was I a good benevolent god, or a punishing wrathful god? I guess to these two disparate groups of ants I was both. I could giveth and taketh away. I worked in strange and mysterious ways. My "Plan" for them was not for them to know, it was something only I could understand.

Theists are much like ants. They credit their unseen imaginary God for their lives, their daily bread and their fortune. They accept His wrath for their sins in the form of disease and disasters. They both praise His benevolence and fear His potential for anger and punishment. That they can do this is the result of having evolved a sophisticated nervous system and an imagination far beyond those of primitive insects. But, to the ants' credit they would, if they could, at least have been worshiping an observable carbon-based life form.

Advantage: Ants.

96

Following God's Orders: How Far Would They Go?

27 Feb 2009

In Genesis 22 God tells Abraham to take his only son, Isaac, and kill him as a sacrifice.

Abraham, devout man that he is, dutifully deceives his family and takes his son to the appointed place, ties him up and prepares to slit his throat. Just in the nick of time an angel appears and stays Abraham's hand. A ram stumbles by which Abraham takes as a sign for a substitute for his son's sacrifice. He kills the ram to satisfy God's blood lust. How heartwarming.

Theists will tell you that this was God testing Abraham to ascertain his degree of faith; that he never intended to let Abraham sacrifice his own son. Basically a sick loyalty test. But given that God does lots of killing of children throughout the Bible, either by direct action or through the divinely directed acts of his creations, not the least of which was the planned killing of his own "begotten son," this God's psychotic homicidal bent is not unusual and pretty damn creepy.

Yet, none of this seems to trouble believers in the least. One would imagine it to be a little disconcerting to true believers since they can never know if and when God will command them to do something really crazy, or at least crazy to most of us.

So the question to Christians is this: If God came to you in a dream, a voice, a vision, and commanded you to take little Susie out of her warm bed, away from her Tickle Me Elmo doll, wrap her up in her Dora The Explorer blanket, take her into the garage and slit her little throat with your Ginsu knife, what would you do?

Now, now ... spare me the protestations of: *"But He wouldn't do that!"* Or the ever popular: *"But that was the God of the Old Testament, there's a new covenant."* Stop! He has done it in the past, and could again, it's the same Being. Hells bells, God killed His own son didn't He? And if He dissolved the "old covenant" with the Jews as Christians claim, what's to stop him from disowning the new covenant, and reissuing a third covenant on a whim?

Nowhere does it say that God is bound by any rule book from reverting to His pre-first century CE personality traits anytime He damn well pleases. Hey, He's God! If He reneges on an agreement, as He has already done, what are they going to do – sue Him? Besides, the "new covenant" was a reiteration of Mosaic Law, and was with "the house of Israel" aka the Jews, not with you "goyim," no matter what kind of scriptural hijacking Christians try. Heck, God allows kids to be killed by the thousands daily. Your kid isn't that special. Besides, who are we to know God's mind or reasoning? After all He transcends man's ability to fully comprehend Him or His actions ... or so the faithful like to say.

That said, let's deal with this head on and drop the theists' self-serving attempts to squirm out of the dilemma with word games, apologetics escape clauses and wishful thinking.

Would a devout Christian, a true believer, kill his/ her own child if they believed God ordered it? If not, does this mean they would intentionally defy God, don't trust God, or would they suspend belief in God because the act is too terrible to comprehend or commit? Or would they trust their God, and go through with it in the hopes of a last minute angelic reprieve, for some divine purpose they cannot know?

Here's my assessment: If they aren't *completely* insane they would let Susie live, take their chances with eternal damnation, and immediately seek the services of a mental health professional. If they *are completely* insane Susie gets served up as God's sushi, as so many deluded Christian parents have done so many times before. Either way they are imbalanced. It's just a matter of degree.

97

Natural Disasters: A Believer's Dilemma

04 March 2009

I posed this question to a devout believer and Creationist: "If God created the Earth, and God is a loving God, why does he kill his innocent loving creations, many of whom are devout believers, with tornados, hurricanes and earthquakes?"

He replies: *"God does not cause or control tornados, hurricanes, or earthquakes. They are a natural result of climate and the movement of tectonic plates."*

"I see" I replied. "So basically one of two things are in play here: Either God erred by creating a defective planet that He did not foresee would continuously kill His innocent creations time and time again, and now can't fix it – thus He is neither omniscient or omnipotent but is a flawed and imperfect designer/creator; OR God intentionally created these conditions, or permits these defects to continue to exist, because He is a blood-thirsty psychopathic thing that enjoys seeing mass death and destruction."

Presented with this dilemma, the good Christian was cornered. But in typical theist style he reaches down deep and comes up with this gem: *"God is a loving God who created a loving world for his creations."* Insert my blank stare here.

A theist who recognizes that the planet's natural disasters are the result of climatic and geologic events is a good thing, a step into reality. But he couples it with crediting a Supreme Being for the planet's creation and all its workings. Thus, when faced with the conflicting dilemma of naturalism and supernaturalism he opts out, abandoning all reason and discourse to a disconnected off-point hackneyed platitude.

But, what else could he do? When we use logic and their defective fables against them in debate, they have nothing but faith and foolishness in defense. Well, at least he didn't invoke "Free Will!" or cry "Context!"

98

Islam's [In]famous Respect for Women

09 March 2009

Recently there was a news report of an American Muslim businessman in upstate New York who cut off his wife's head. What prompted this gruesome act is still unclear, although his wife had recently filed for divorce.

The husband and his wife had been American citizens for years. In all outward respects they appeared to have fully embraced Western culture and the American lifestyle. Mr. Hassan started a Muslim TV station in 2004, popular with US Muslims. His purpose was to present Americans with a kinder, gentler face of Islam. So much for that.

The same week, a judge in Saudi Arabia sentenced a pregnant woman to one year in jail and one hundred lashes. Her crime? She was gang raped, beaten and left pregnant by her attackers. It seems she was found guilty of adultery for her victimization, even though she wasn't married, because she was outside her home unaccompanied by a male relative, a violation of Saudi Law. In a show of mercy, they won't be administering the flogging until she gives birth to the child.

Last year a thirteen-year-old Somali girl, a victim of rape, was falsely convicted of adultery (a capital crime under Islamic law) and stoned to death by an execution squad of fifty men. A crowd of one thousand gathered in a stadium to watch.

In Iran, a woman was recently blinded by a rejected suitor. The would-be boyfriend poured acid over her head, into her eyes, down her face. She lost sight in both eyes and was horribly scarred. He said he did it because he loved her.

This week in Turkey a woman was murdered by six members of her family; an "honor killing" because she had been raped, which had brought disgrace upon her family.

These obscene miscarriages of justice, acts of horrific vengeance, and perverted logic are not isolated examples. They occur regularly, daily, throughout the Islamic world, and among Muslims in Western countries. Women being beheaded, flogged, stoned to death, imprisoned, murdered by their families, receiving retribution with acid are so commonplace that only a very few find their way into the mainstream media. While most Islamic governments have laws against honor killings (and acid attacks), nevertheless it begs the question of why this horrific violence against women is so wide spread in among Muslims.

Most moderate Muslims (a term that I find paradoxical given their professed majority, yet their deafening silence in response to radical Muslim actions) will say that the Koran neither prescribes nor condones these acts of injustice against women. They will say it isn't a religious issue, it's culturally driven. They are partially correct, partially lying, partially in denial.

The Koran and the Sunna (or Sunnah) comprises the Shari'a, the basis for Islamic Law. The penalty for adultery, for men or women, is death by stoning. The Koran says women are inferior to men, and their husbands have the right to "scourge" them for disobedience. And while honor killings aren't specifically mentioned, most Muslim clerics justify it, thus laws against it are laxly enforced and the penalties for it usually minor. For all intents and purposes, then, it has become part of Islam.

When a religion, and the culture that embraces it, makes women less valued than men; when it imposes penalties more harshly and frequently against them than male adulterers; when it obsesses over women's dress, modesty, and obedience; when it places such a high value on a woman's purity that any loss of purity, whether by choice or by force, renders a family's name forever soiled; and when prescribed punishments for crimes, trespasses, "sins" are uniquely violent even barbaric ... then you have a recipe for institutionalized, sanctioned, abuse of women.

There remains one question that the Thinking should consider. The Old Testament likewise endorsed death for infractions of any number of laws, and the New Testament as well as the Old has many verses that demean the status of women. Yet in the West, in secular countries where the "Judeo-Christian morality" prevails, why do we not see similar excesses? Why does it seem to be a largely Islamic aberration? Because while in the West ethics and morality evolved over time, replacing religious doctrine with secular reasoning, Islamic countries have not evolved, or are still in the process of evolving, albeit at a snails pace. Slavery is still condoned in Chad, Niger, Mali and the Sudan, where the Koran is cited as justification.

Although Islamic countries employ 21st century technology, and control vast portions of petroleum reserves, thus wielding significant influence in the world's economy, that is only the outward face of Islam. For all intents and purposes Islam and the cultures into which it has inculcated its teachings and principles have condemned its people to a seventh century mentality. The losers are freedom loving/peace loving nations, the poor and undereducated Muslims, and Muslim women.

That's the bad news. The worse news is Islam is the fastest growing religion on the planet, and they have an "end times" doctrine of their own. A worse combination is hard to imagine.

99

Geography & Parentage versus Revelation

14 March 2009

Geography (one's place of birth), and the brand of one's parent's religion are undeniably the single greatest influence on a theist's particular flavor of superstition.

This is a fact based on simple observation and evidence. For example, more than 80% of the population of India is Hindu. They didn't suddenly decide to become Hindu by random chance, or by evaluating every other religion on Earth and making an informed decision. India has been a seat of Hinduism for 2600 years or more. Ninety percent of the world's one billion+ Hindus reside in India and Nepal. Thus, when a child is born in India, there is a high probability that his parents are Hindu and overwhelming likelihood they will raise him as a Hindu.

A Christian was espousing the usual insipid nonsense about Christianity being the "one true religion." Further, that he had chosen Christianity because it was revealed to him by God. I asked where he was from and if his parents were likewise believers. He was from Alabama, and he assured me his parents were devout Christians, or as he put it *"They are Saved."* I posited that if he had been born in India, to Indian parents who practice Hinduism, it's more than likely that he'd believe Hinduism was the one true religion, and would scoff at and dismiss Christianity and its dogma. Thus, it isn't revelation that made him Christian, it was an accident of geography and parentage that decided for him what the "one true" religion is.

Using that famous Christian openness to logic and reality he retorts with, *"No, I still would have been a Christian."* I tried to get him to explain in logical terms how if he had been born to Hindu parents, in India he would avoid having been indoctrinated into their prevailing belief system. All I received for my effort was ,*"You wouldn't understand."* Well, that solves that problem.

So in the absence of a worthy theist apologist, I shall venture a guess as to what he would propose would have caused a child born in India to Hindu parents to become a Christian. It works like this: Jesus would have recognized him as a person MEANT to be Christian, and thus would have implanted in him a "Christian gene," or some such predisposition toward Christianity. Of course, this would mean that this particular child, having been uniquely selected from among nine hundred million Indian Hindus, was the "Chosen Indian of Jesus".

This then sets him above the one billion+ Hindus Jesus doesn't deem worthy of hypnotizing, enticing, or otherwise receiving His "revealed" singular Truth. All those others would be ignored by Jesus, and are condemned to Hell for not abandoning their historic

Hindu faith and coming to the Lord independently, without His divine intervention. It would infer he would be the hand-selected of God among all others. Obviously this is something our Christian friend was not prepared to proffer or defend in an open chat room. Better to leave it at *"You wouldn't understand."*

But, we do understand. We understand that to people like him supernaturalism, denial of fact and abandonment of reason in defense of a belief always trumps real world logic and experience.

100

Religiosity and Intelligence

14 March 2009

In the spring of 1986, *Free Inquiry* a respected magazine that promotes secular humanism and rational thinking, published a detailed article entitled *"The Effect of Intelligence on Religious Faith."* Contained within that article were sixteen studies conducted from 1927 through 1980 that examined college students' degree of religiosity and their intellectual ability as measured by test scores and grades.

Of the sixteen studies, thirteen of them, 81%, showed an inverse correlation between religiosity and intelligence. That is, the aggregate scores were consistently highest among the least religious and non-believers, and lowest among the more religious/most religious. While three studies reported no statistical difference between the groups, not a single one of the studies reported higher intelligence in the religious groups versus the less religious/non-believer groups.

A list of those studies follows for those who would like to research this further:

Thomas Howells, 1927
Hilding Carlsojn, 1933
Abraham Franzblau, 1934
Thomas Symington, 1935
Vernon Jones, 1938
A. R. Gilliland, 1940 *(no statistical difference)*
Donald Gragg, 1942
Brown and Love, 1951
Michael Argyle, 1958
Jeffrey Hadden, 1963 *(no statistical difference)*
Young, Dustin and Holtzman, 1966
James Trent, 1967 *(no statistical difference)*
C. Plant and E. Minium, 1967
Robert Wuthnow, 1978
Norman Poythress, 1975
Wiebe and Fleck, 1980

The results of the Poythress ('75) study were typical of the majority findings. They tracked SAT scores of religious students compared to three levels of non-belief/anti-religiosity. It showed that as religious belief declined/ anti-religiosity increased SAT scores increased commensurately. The religious student group average SAT scores were 10% lower than the most anti-religious student group.

Another example, the Brown and Love ('51) study, tracked controlled test scores. Believers' averaged 19% lower average test scores than did non-believers.

I have discussed in another chapter the fact that the most eminent scientists in the US and Great Britain, members of The National Academy of Science, and the Royal Society, have much lower rates of religious belief than does the general population of either country.

So when we take all this data into account, what conclusion can we draw? Well, we cannot infer that all atheists are smarter than all theists. That would be an easily falsified assumption. But we can deduce by a preponderance of corroborating results from scientifically conducted studies that on the aggregate atheists are more intelligent than believers.

The reason for this is not difficult to surmise. People who can best access problems using reason, fact and logic use those same attributes to analyze/examine the claims of theistic belief. When they do they conclude those claims to be lacking. People with lesser degrees of those attributes are least likely to apply critical thinking to religious claims and are more inclined to accept them at face.

The evidence for this is overwhelming and not a recent observation. Celsus, a second century Greek writer, was a careful observer of the early Christian movement and critic of it. Among his many observations are the following:

"… *the following are the rules laid down by them* [Christian proselytizers] . *Let no one come to us who has been instructed, or who is wise or prudent (for such qualifications are deemed evil by us); but if there be any ignorant, or unintelligent, or uninstructed, or foolish persons, let them come with confidence. By which words, acknowledging that such individuals are worthy of their God, they manifestly show that they desire and are able to gain over only the silly, and the mean, and the stupid, with women and children.*"

"*Only foolish and low individuals, and persons devoid of perception, and slaves, and women, and children, of whom the teachers of the divine word wish to make converts…*"[1]

---

[1] http://www.bluffton.edu/~humanities/1/celsus.htm

The least educated, least discerning, most ignorant and gullible are those least likely to challenge and question, and more likely to blindly accept faith over fact. This is just as true of Islam, the fastest growing religion in the world thanks to its appeal to the most undereducated and hopeless inhabitants of the Third World.

Here's a tip – if you see people who are babbling mindlessly in tongues, or handling snakes as they dance around praising Jesus; or proclaiming the Earth to be 6,000 years old; or crawling on their hands and knees to be touched by a faith healer; or allowing themselves to be ceremonially crucified in honor of their savior; or attesting to the End being near; feel comfortable giving good odds and betting a month's salary that none of them are brain surgeons, rocket scientists, or Mensa members. It's money in the bank.

101

Ok Atheists, Your Turn:
An Annoying Atheist Trait

18 March 2009

In a well structured atheist forum a valued and active participant posted an informal poll which simply posed the question: *"How likely is it that God exists?"*

He structured the percentage options in descending increments from 100% to 0% likelihood. Checking one of the ratings entered your vote. I voted "< 1% " (I would never say zero percent since that would infer absolutism; thus I always allow for say 0.000001% chance of some deity's existence; in other words about as likely as a monkey flying out of my colon.)

This seemingly simple question was, I thought, adequately clear to permit a simple response from this community of mostly atheists and agnostics. I couldn't have been more mistaken.

What followed were twenty replies asking the pollster to clarify what he meant by "God." Is this limited to the universally recognized definition of God? Does it encompass definitions that would include Spinoza's

god and/or the god of Einstein which was a metaphor-
ical god? Define "exist!" Define "likely!" Does <1%
qualify as > 0%, and if so, why not just have >0% as an
option instead of <1%? (I may be misstating here, as
I zoned out and lost interest in that particular line of
interrogation). Participants were even arguing among
themselves over the definitions and rating possibilities.
It went on like this ad nauseam.

I find it telling, and annoying, that so many of the
responses focused on hair splitting of word intentions
and nit picking over the scale gradient. They seemed
so driven toward a level of exactitude that it all but
rendered the original poll question irrelevant, simply
not worth bothering with. Maybe as Free Thinkers we
are sometimes guilty of ignoring the simplest and least
convoluted approach, instead making it as complex as
we possibly can. For example, I can just imagine this
exchange:

Coworker: *"Geeze ... it's raining hard outside isn't it?"*

Atheist: *"Oh?? DEFINE 'hard'. Furthermore, your reference to 'outside' is superfluous, since unless we had a struc-
tural fault, aka roof leak, meteorologically speaking it doesn't
rain 'inside'."*

Coworker: *"Hey, here's a thought, why don't you go fuck
yourself."*

Now, don't misunderstand me. I'm not suggesting
we dumb down, or suppress our desire, our innate
need to eliminate ambiguity. We are after all analytical, thinking people; it's what sets us apart from the
unquestioning credulous theists. I'm saying that maybe there is a time and place for exactitude, and a time
to just answer the damn question lest we be branded
"anal retentive jerks" along with our preferred title of
"Godless heathens."

102

Christian Apologetics: Knowledge and Intellect Not Required

24 March 2009

There are websites, overpaid charlatans, and wandering internet Christians who are dedicated to apologetics, the defense or "proof" of Christianity to win converts. It's an age-old practice going back to the 2nd century.

One of the earliest Christian apologists was Justin Martyr who lived from 100 to 165 CE. His efforts were directed mostly toward the Roman hierarchy, and the Greek philosophers. One of the most famous and laughable defenses of Christianity was his explanation of why there were pagan predecessor gods to Jesus who shared very similar life stories and attributes. Justin claimed those gods were put in men's minds by Satan in order to confuse man in preparation for Jesus' coming. I imagine that got a chuckle from the educated Roman senators and Hellenistic Philosophers.

In the 1930's a British journalist, pen named Frank Morison, claimed he was raised a Christian but was skeptical of the resurrection myth. He embarked on detailed study of the scripture and visited the Holy Land. In his book *Who Moved the Stone?* he came to the conclusion that Jesus' resurrection was indeed real. Why? What lead him to this conclusion? His bottom line was this: *Because there were guards all around the tomb, and after visiting the supposed tomb it was clear that it would have been impossible for anyone else to move the stone blocking the entrance.* Thus, he "proved" the veracity of the scripture by using <u>the very same scripture</u> as the sole source of information. Now there's a journalistic investigator for you.

These days, Ray Comfort is among the most visible Christian apologists. A complete lack of understanding of scientific principles and evolutionary theory don't stand in the way of his trying to discredit them in favor of Creationism. What he lacks in real knowledge he makes up, falsely attributing his laughably inane misrepresentations of evolutionary theory to Darwin. Comfort is best remembered for proffering that the banana is proof of God; for why else would it (I paraphrase Ray) "... *fit so perfectly in our hands, and have such a convenient wrapper?*" Ray doesn't like being asked about pineapples.

Recently I heard a particularly vapid would-be apologist exclaim that Christianity is the "one True religion." His proof rested in the fact that C.S. Lewis, some obscure British jurist, and other 19th and 20th century personages of some minor notoriety abandoned skepticism and became devout Christians. To his limited thought processes this was evidence of the veracity of Christianity. All things being equal, the fact that more people are leaving Christianity than are joining it, preferring to trust reality and naturalism or even Islam, should be considered valid evidence for Christianity's falsehood. But that doesn't occur to apologists, or at least not to the really bad ones.

When faced with the mathematical impossibility of millions of animal species, along with their food and feces, being crammed into a boat with a finite volume incapable of housing them; a would-be apologist suggested that *"God may have made those animals all babies, and so they didn't take up as much room, and maybe they didn't have to eat or poop."* Now there's a solid foundation for intelligent discourse.

What these five examples of defenders of the faith all have in common is this: They rely on attempts at knowledge and intellect to support their belief. However, their lack of both attributes work against them. Genuine apologists don't try to match their understanding of science/scientific theory, the natural world with educated advocates of science and reality. They don't attempt isolated examples of "evidence" that can be dismissed as inventive subjective woulda-coulda, or falsified by anyone capable of looking past their nose.

Genuine Christian apologists tell their disciples that to be effective in spreading the "Truth" of Christianity and to bring non-believers to Jesus, they have to abandon knowledge and intellect, and depend only on faith. They say they must "rely on God, not knowledge." They recognize that knowledge is an ineffective tool, cautioning them that "Study should never replace the power of God." [1] And of course they are correct. A belief system that has no concrete evidence for its doctrine; no qualitative or quantitative proofs; that cannot support its myth and supernaturalism with real world example is destined to be discredited when

---

[1] http://www.allaboutgod.com/christian-apologetics.htm

facing opposition from natural world evidence, proofs and genuine knowledge. They recognize that it is tantamount to their bringing a pen knife to a gun fight.

What's interesting about their advice, what's so telling about their religion, is that they are endorsing and promulgating the same thing the early Christian Church did – the downplaying of study, discrediting of knowledge and demonization of intellectual growth. Why? Because they know that their religion's continuation, its very existence, is predicated on not attracting the most intelligent, most analytical, least credulous to their ranks. That would be a waste of time. It has, is, and always will be geared toward convincing and attracting the least educated, most credulous and gullible.

You'll recognize the "real" apologists when you see them. They're the ones who don't try and come up with half-baked retorts to scientific evidence. They're the ones who, when they make a religious pronouncement offered up as fact, and you ask them for proof, will answer with something akin to: *"Proof? Proof??? I don't need no steenking proof!! I have faith."*

103

Religiosity, Mental Illness, and Molestation: An Unholy Connection

29 March 2009

I met a believer online, let's call him "Adam," who introduced himself to me as *"… gay, promiscuous, OCD* [Obsessive Compulsive Disorder] *and bipolar."* Too much info from someone whose name I don't even know. Then it got worse. It seems he was molested by a priest as a child and attributes all of his "issues" to that event. His condition is so severe he had to drop out of college. To make matters worse, his parents reject him for his homosexuality. The fact that he shared all this with a complete stranger was a warning sign.

Evidently the point of his divulging this was to set the stage for proclaiming that I, as an avowed atheist, am a "fraud;" that I can't possibly be an atheist, since *"everyone has faith,"* even him; even after what happened to him at the hands of that priest, even with his unhappy life and afflictions. I assured him that I was indeed an atheist, but this only served to enflame him. He became progressively more irate, agitated and hostile. It was bizarre. I left him to his ranting.

This exchange prompted me to wonder about the relationship between religion and mental illness. While I was familiar with hyper-religiosity, a clinically accepted term for certain schizophrenics who become extremely obsessed with religion, to the point of delusion, I was curious as to what research has been done on religiosity and lesser degrees of mental illness. I didn't have to look far to find there exists a plethora of medical studies that show positive correlation between high religiosity, OCD, bipolar disorder and childhood sexual abuse.

One study published in *Psychiatric Research* concluded that while religion does not cause OCD, people with multiple obsessions will tend to exhibit higher frequency of religious obsession.

http://linkinghub.elsevier.com/retrieve/pii/S016517810 1003109

In an article on bipolar disease, high religiosity is exhibited as a secondary, less prevalent symptom, appearing in 39% of bipolar patients. Hyper sexuality appears in 57% of patients (explaining Adam's description of himself as promiscuous).

http://www.medscape.com/viewarticle/412807_2

Wiki reports that bipolar disorder symptoms include irritability, escalating to rage, and hyper-religiosity. *http://en.wikipedia.org/wiki/Manic_episode.* This is confirmed by medical authorities such as the *Nelson Textbook of Pediatrics.*

In fact, there is a Christian website that not only recognizes the bipolar connection to religiosity, it counsels bipolar believers on how to differentiate between religiosity and spirituality that is "fruitful" and that which is driven by their disease. *http://www.chastitysf.com/bipolar.htm*

Finally, and most telling is this: Studies show that there is a "significant relationship" between childhood sexual abuse and religiosity. Abused children are substantially more likely to become religious than non-abused children. One might easily conclude that Adam's religiosity isn't *in spite* of his being abused ... he was condemned to religiosity by *his abuse.*

The Journal of Child Sexual Abuse published the authoritative work on this subject. *http://eric. ed.gov/ERICWebPortal/custom/portlets/recordDetails/de- tailmini.jsp?_nfpb=true&_&ERICExtSearch_Search- Value_0=EJ564932&ERICExtSearch_SearchType_ 0=no&accno=EJ564932*

This is just a sampling. The facts I present here are corroborated by many medical authorities' websites; hundreds of them.

Adam's attributing his homosexuality, OCD and bipolar disorder to his abuse by that priest is likely his own rationalization. There is a clear inference, however, that his mental disorders, combined with his sexual abuse, produced his less than "fruitful", highly aggressive form of religiosity.

But what's even more interesting is this: If you do a search for *"atheism and mental illness, bipolar, OCD"* there is not a single study, not a single link, that associates mental disorder with non-belief or vise versa. The only thing it does show are people who were once atheist who, as a result of their disorder, "converted" to belief.

What does this all mean vis-à-vis the religious and their mental stability? It certainly does *not* mean that all believers are insane, any more than all atheists are sane. What it demonstrates is that the relationship between mental instability and being religious is undeniable. Should any of us be surprised?

104

Religious Indoctrination: Brainwashing, or Just a Rinse and Set?

02 April 2009

brainwashing

*I*ndoctrination that forces people to abandon their beliefs in favor of another set of beliefs. **Usually associated with military and political interrogation and religious conversion,** brainwashing attempts, through prolonged stress, to break down an individual's physical and mental defenses. Brainwashing **techniques range from vocal persuasion and threats to punishment,** physical deprivation, mind-altering drugs, and severe physical torture.

The American Heritage®

So, is indoctrinating a child to a "belief" brainwashing? Strictly speaking, a person would need to hold a perspective, a view, a "belief" that is in opposition to the indoctrinator's preferred thinking. To that extent, a child who holds no preconceived notion, no perspective, and no view and is indoctrinated into the parent's belief system might not be strictly considered a victim of brainwashing.

However, if we take the position that <u>not</u> having a belief in the supernatural/God/gods is by default atheism at birth, then the argument might be made that the parents are indeed indoctrinating, inducing, forcing abandonment of lack of belief (aka atheism) for a preferred supernatural religious belief.

Some might take issue with the word forcing. But force comes in a variety of forms. It doesn't have to mean physical force. Among the many definitions of force is administration of power by one who holds authority over one who has no power; to exercise persuasive power, to convince.

But beyond that, what can be more forceful, more intimidating, than to tell a child that failure to believe like the parents do will result in an eternity of pain and unbearable anguish in a hideously fearful place, and separation from the parents after death? Talk about force and coercion!

I'd proffer that unless a child is presented with the alternatives to the parents' expressed religious belief; provided with the variety of options in variance to that specific belief; and given the option of no belief ... and to have it presented dispassionately, without prejudice, fear, threat or undue influence, then indeed parental indoctrination of a child into their preferred belief system IS brainwashing.

It is as much brainwashing as a Palestinian child being indoctrinated by his parents to hate and want to kill Jews. Whether it is a mindset of good or evil is in the eye of the believer; it doesn't change the fact that it is inducing a belief, a view, that otherwise might not have been the child's own given the various options.

When, as a child, my eldest son asked me if there was a god my answer was *"A lot of people think so, some people don't."* When he asked if I believed in God I told him *"I don't, but your Mom does."* When he asked if <u>he</u> believed in God my reply was *"You'll have to decide for yourself when you are older."* He was satisfied with that. No threat, no dogma, no force or indoctrination of a malleable mind ill-equipped to reason, weigh and assess rationally.

Unfortunaltely, theist parents just aren't comfortable allowing their child the "free will" to decide. It's the parent's will or else. If that's not brainwashing nothing is.

105

"Atheism is the View of the Feeble and the Gullible!"

05 April 2009

That remarkable statement was actually made by a fundamentalist Christian.

It's difficult for most people to fathom that kind of convoluted logic knowing what we know about what makes one an atheist. But there it was, in black and white.

Free Thinkers value evidence. We are slow to accept concepts proffered as fact without it. I don't know any atheists who blindly accept as genuine fortune tellers, ghosts, poltergeist, mind readers, or any of the vast assortments of fictional beasts that are alleged to haunt the woods and oceans and lakes. That's not to say we wouldn't if presented with enough proof to make the reality of their existence evident. It's just that there has never been any satisfactory proof, and lots of evidence to the contrary.

Similarly, while we are interested in radical new scientific theories, most of us are skeptical and don't jump on board until we gather more information, see the data peer-reviewed and vetted, and are provided with corroborating evidence that gives the theory credence. Even then, we do not apply "absolute" acceptance. Thus, by definition, atheists are the exact antithesis of gullible. I won't even bother to broach the rhetorical charge of "feeble."

Every few years a self-appointed Christian shaman predicts the End Times, the Rapture, and thousands of devout sheep baa their praise, give away their belongings, quit their jobs and await the Second Coming, only to have it pass uneventfully. They pray for rain, for gas prices to fall, for peace to come to the earth, for Aunt Jane to be cured from her brain dead condition. Yet when these things don't happen they still retain belief in prayer. They wave their hands and praise the Lord, watching fake healers cure their fake co-conspirators. They believe Satan planted fossils to confuse us; that demons exist and can possess people; that angels fly around; that dead things come to life, etc., all with as much evidence as exists for the Loch Ness Monster. This they consider discriminating.

Of course, if you were to tell a Christian you have a talking mouse in your pocket ... THEN they'd demand evidence, proof. You can't put anything over on them, after all there were no talking mice in the Bible, only talking snakes and talking donkeys.

So how can a theist make the patently absurd claim that *"atheism is the view of the feeble and the gullible?"* To fundamentalists the Bible is the actual or inspired word of God. It's not a debatable matter; it's a matter of faith. To them the Bible is both historically and scientifically accurate, for how could God deceive or make errors, or permit errors to be made in his name?

Ignore the pesky overwhelming scientific proofs that contradict the Bible, faith is faith and that's that, man's knowledge is subservient to God's word. If this is the mindset of the unschooled, unthinking religiously fanatical then it is apparent to them that atheists, who accept theories in opposition to God's word, have been fooled. Never mind that our acceptance of these scientific facts are based on detailed analysis and familiarity with a preponderance of physical evidence founded on natural principles; corroborated, tested and repeatable data that disproves ancient fable … we have been deceived, bamboozled.

Some Christians say we are led astray by science and the secular world. The most impaired adherents will credit Satan with our "deception." But in either case we atheists have clearly shown our gullibility by accepting reality, evidence and proofs resulting from many years of scientific examination, discoveries, and technological advancements; while simultaneously rejecting the unsupportable "obvious Truth" of scripture.

This is what passes for logic, critical thinking, among the wackiest fundamentalist apologists. This is why his statement about atheists being feeble and gullible makes sense, but only to him and his similarly impaired brethren. But then the fundie surprised me and offered this unexpected admission: *"Christianity isn't the thinking man's religion."* For once we were in agreement.

Afterword

Religion has always been with us. It will be with us for many years to come even though it is destined, in my opinion, for extinction at the hands of reason. A recent Associated Press story reported that non-belief in the United States has grown by 82% from 1990 to 2008, while Christianity has declined 10%. If that rate of growth in non-belief is sustained, religion in the United States will be largely just a bad memory in sixty years. As an anti-theist activist, I am dedicated to help speed its demise, albeit I will not live long enough to celebrate its disappearance.

In an age of nuclear, chemical and biological weaponry, the world has more at risk than the burnings of a few thousand heretics, or the destruction of a few million who fell under the sword and siege engines of religious fanatics. The potential for mass extinction is real; a manmade Armageddon at the hands of religious extremists who anxiously await the "End Times" and have no compunctions about helping to bring it about. To deny that fact, to ignore it, to be complacent, is to be an unwitting accomplice.

To not be outraged, to not speak against those who seek to force their religious precepts on others at the expense of peoples freedoms, is to be a co-conspirator in the subjugation of those freedoms; your freedoms or those of your neighbor.

Yet, as theists shrink in numbers and influence throughout the industrialized world, its strongest proponents will not go quietly into that good night. They will rail against secularism, decry their loss of power, and seek to recruit and rally the faithful with promises of *their* reward and *our* eternal damnation; invoking biblical reference to the war between the forces of light and darkness. Whether driven by genuine religious zealotry, or by profit motive, these fundamentalists mean to make us into their image or die trying. I have no problem with their dying trying; I have a problem with them making any of us die with them.

In the Third World, where Islam is on the rise – often in its most virulent form – we face an even more difficult challenge as superstition and dangerous doctrine blend with under-education and ancient cultural imperatives that defy displacement by scientific proofs, reality, logic and modernity. As the products of this religious infirmity immigrate to industrialized nations the danger it represents to the most basic freedom, freedom of speech and expression, is threatened. Already European countries whose Muslim populations are steadily growing are truncating the freedoms of their native populations out of fear of Islamic power. The imposition of laws demanding "cultural sensitivity," political correctness, and self-censorship under penalty of the law have been adopted by Great Britain, parts of Scandinavia and other Western European countries.

These laws are in response to threats and intimidation, both veiled and overt, by an intolerant philosophy and insulated culture that laughs at the Infidel's acquiescence and sees it as a weakness – and an opportunity. Parts of Europe have already begun the process of surrendering their birthright. They are losing their culture to Islamic fundamentalism.

The responsibility of us the thinking, who will not succumb to religious ignorance and intolerance, is to speak out against any attempts to abridge our freedom from without or from within. When the time comes in the United States that drawing a picture of the Prophet Mohammed becomes a prosecutable hate crime we will know where we are heading. A phrase often attributed to Benjamin Franklin says it all: *"Those who would give up Essential Liberty to purchase a little Temporary Safety deserve neither Liberty nor Safety."* Words to live by.

BSC aka Dromedary Hump

Recommended Organizations

The following organizations are at the forefront of the fight to retain the separation of church and state; promote reason and free inquiry; and are dedicated to the protection of the individual's right of freedom *of* and *from* religion. I strongly recommend them to anyone, theist or atheist, who endorses those precepts:

Freedom from Religion Foundation
PO Box 750
Madison WI 53701
http://www.ffrf.org/index.php

Americans United for Separation of Church and State
518 C Street NE
Washington, DC 20002
http://www.au.org/site/PageServer

Military Religious Freedom Foundation
13170-B Central Ave. SE
Suite 255
Albuquerque, NM 87123
http://militaryreligiousfreedom.org/

American Civil Liberties Union (ACLU)

125 Broad Street, 18th Floor
New York, NY 10004
http://www.aclu.org/

Center for Inquiry
P.O. Box 741
Amherst, NY 14226
info@centerforinquiry.net

Recommended Readings

Non-Fiction

Separation of Church and State:
> *God on Trial: Dispatches from America's Religious Battle-fields*, Peter Irons
> *Piety & Politics*, Rev. Barry Lynn

Atheist Perspectives:
> *The God Delusion*, Richard Dawkins
> *The End of Faith*, Sam Harris
> *god is not Great*, Christopher Hitchens
> *The Portable Atheist*, Christopher Hitchens

Modernist Christian Perspective:
> *Why Christianity Must Change or Die*, Bishop John Shelby Spong

Biblical Scholarship & Criticism:
> *The Incredible Shrinking Son of Man*, Robert M. Price
> *Deconstructing Jesus*, Robert M. Price
> *God Against the Gods*, Jonathan Kirsch
> *Misquoting Jesus*, Bart D. Ehrman
> *Who Wrote the Bible?*, Richard Elliott Friedman

History of Religious Injustice, Intolerance, Fanaticism:
> *Constantine's Sword*, James Carroll
> *Out of the Flames*, Lawrence & Nancy Goldstone

Under the Banner of Heaven: A Story of Violent Faith, Jon Krakauer

A Delusion of Satan, Frances Hill

Fiction

The Holy Bible, King James Version (KJV); New Revised Standard Version (NRSV), et al.

About the Author

DROMEDARY HUMP is a lifelong activist in the culture war between theist demagoguery and Free Thinkers, and a frequent outspoken contributor and guest columnist to various newspapers and periodicals. He lives in New Hampshire with his saintly and much-put-upon Episcopal wife of thirty-nine years and their two atheist dogs. His blog *The Atheist Camel* can be accessed at http://atheistcamel.blogspot.com/.

Made in the USA
Lexington, KY
19 February 2010